word alive

n-depth Small Group
ible Studies

STUDY
GUIDE

DANIEL

daring faith in dangerous times

Case Van Kempen

Daniel

FAITH
ALIVE®
Christian Resources

Grand Rapids, Michigan

Cover photo: Taxi

Word Alive: In-depth Small Group Bible Studies

Daniel: Daring Faith in Dangerous Times (Study Guide), © 2003 by Faith Alive
Christian Resources, 2850 Kalamazoo Ave. SE, Grand Rapids, MI 49560. All
rights reserved. With the exception of brief excerpts for review purposes, no part
of this book may be reproduced in any manner whatsoever without written
permission from the publisher. Printed in the United States of America on
recycled paper.

We welcome your comments. Call us at 1-800-333-8300 or e-mail us at
editors@faithaliveresources.org.

www.FaithAliveResources.org

ISBN 978-1-56212-981-1

10 9 8 7 6 5 4 3 2

Contents

Introduction

"Daniel in the Lions' Den," "Three Men in a Fiery Furnace," "The Handwriting on the Wall"—just the names of these stories remind many of us of how familiar we once were with stories about the exiled prophet Daniel and his three friends. When we were children, Daniel's life was the stuff of our Sunday school lessons, our songs, and even some of our coloring books. Daniel was one of the "heroes of the Old Testament."

As adults, though, we rarely turn to this important book of prophecy. Mixed in with the stories still told in Sunday school are several extravagant visions of an unfolding future for the Babylonians and the Medes and Persians. The later chapters of the book are filled with still more dream and vision stories, describing outrageous beasts, warrior angels, and world-conquering armies. It can seem hard to imagine that these could have anything to do with the world of today.

Has it, in fact, been a while since you've been through the book of Daniel? If so, you may be surprised to discover how timely Daniel's message is. Consider these examples: Do you often find yourself standing at a counter where a clerk asks, "Do you want fries with that?" If you do, Daniel's dietary decisions may be a helpful reminder about making healthy choices—or, more important, about making obedient ones. Do you ever wonder if a handful of Christians can make a difference against the onslaught of immorality portrayed on television or in movies today? Maybe Shadrach, Meshach, and Abednego—who refused to bow down to Nebuchadnezzar's golden statue—can convince us that yes, we can. Does the fear of terrorism or what seems to be constant international conflict cause you to worry about your personal safety? Daniel's clear visions about the rise and fall of nations can assure you that God is fully in control.

From beginning to end, Daniel's prophecy reveals that the one true God steers not only the course of nature and nations but also the lives of every person in history. No one's life is too small to be kept safely in God's hands, and no empire is too large to exceed God's grasp. As Daniel put it,

> "Praise be to the name of God for ever and ever;
> wisdom and power are his.
> He changes the times and seasons;
> he sets up kings and deposes them.
> He gives wisdom to the wise
> and knowledge to the discerning.
> He reveals deep and hidden things;
> he knows what lies in darkness,
> and light dwells with him."   (Dan. 2:20-22)

May God's Holy Spirit guide and bless you as you study the book of Daniel, and may a faith like Daniel's be with all who read his inspired words.

—Case Van Kempen

Case Van Kempen, author of this study guide and the accompanying leader's guide, is a minister in the Reformed Church in America. He has served churches in Clymer, New York; Franklin Lakes, New Jersey; and Holland, Michigan. He and his wife, Leigh, currently live in Holland, and they have three children: Abigail, Peter, and Paul. Case is also the author of *Hard Questions People Ask About the Christian Faith* (Faith Alive, 2002).

*What happens,
or doesn't happen,
when we trust
and obey?*

1

DANIEL 1

Strangers in a Strange Land

In a Nutshell
Our introduction to the story of Daniel and his companions begins with a brief history of the time in which they lived. As we learn how they came to be exiled from their homes in Judah and underwent training to serve the king of Babylon, we can see how God faithfully provided for them to be obedient to the true King of their lives.

Daniel 1
¹In the third year of the reign of Jehoiakim king of Judah, Nebuchadnezzar king of Babylon came to Jerusalem and besieged it. ²And the Lord delivered Jehoiakim king of Judah into his hand, along with some of the articles from the temple of God. These he carried off to the temple of his god in Babylonia and put in the treasure house of his god.

³Then the king ordered Ashpenaz, chief of his court officials, to bring in some of the Israelites from the royal family and the nobility—⁴young men without any physical defect, handsome, showing aptitude for every kind of learning, well informed, quick to understand, and qualified to serve in the king's palace. He was to teach them the language and literature of the Babylonians. ⁵The king assigned them a daily amount of food and wine from the king's table. They were to be trained for three years, and after that they were to enter the king's service.

⁶Among these were some from Judah: Daniel, Hananiah, Mishael and Azariah.

⁷The chief official gave them new names: to Daniel, the name Belteshazzar; to Hananiah, Shadrach; to Mishael, Meshach; and to Azariah, Abednego.

⁸But Daniel resolved not to defile himself with the royal food and wine, and he asked the chief official for permission not to defile himself this way. ⁹Now God had caused the official to show favor and sympathy to Daniel, ¹⁰but the official told Daniel, "I am afraid of my lord the king, who has assigned your food and drink. Why should he see you looking worse than the other young men your age? The king would then have my head because of you."

¹¹Daniel then said to the guard whom the chief official had appointed over Daniel, Hananiah, Mishael and Azariah, ¹²"Please test your servants for ten days: Give us nothing but vegetables to eat and water to drink. ¹³Then compare our appearance with that of the young men who eat the royal food, and treat your servants in accordance with what you see." ¹⁴So he agreed to this and tested them for ten days.

15At the end of the ten days they looked healthier and better nourished than any of the young men who ate the royal food. 16So the guard took away their choice food and the wine they were to drink and gave them vegetables instead.

17To these four young men God gave knowledge and understanding of all kinds of literature and learning. And Daniel could understand visions and dreams of all kinds.

18At the end of the time set by the king to bring them in, the chief official pre-sented them to Nebuchadnezzar. 19The king talked with them, and he found none equal to Daniel, Hananiah, Mishael and Azariah; so they entered the king's service. 20In every matter of wisdom and under-standing about which the king questioned them, he found them ten times better than all the magicians and enchanters in his whole kingdom.

21And Daniel remained there until the first year of King Cyrus.

Names, Dates, and Places

There's no way to get around it. If we want to understand the stories, visions, and prophecies of Daniel, we have to under-stand something about the history of the time in which Daniel lived. If we don't know the difference between an Egyptian Ptolemy and a Syrian Seleucid, we won't be able to make much sense of the vivid imagery revealed to Daniel to describe those ancient dynasties.

But understanding the setting of Daniel doesn't require a Ph.D. in antiquities. If you can remember who Napoleon was, if you know who gave a famous speech at Gettysburg, or if you can tell which country was often described as a great "bear" during the Cold War, you'll be able to grasp the basic history and images found in the book of Daniel.

Before we get to the history itself, though, let's make a mental note of why it's so important: *God's Word was given to specific peo-ple living in specific times and places*. While the underlying message of salvation is timeless, the specific circumstances in which God's Word is revealed tell us a great deal about that eternal message.

For example, imagine reading Abraham Lincoln's Gettysburg Address if you knew nothing about the American Civil War. A few phrases might have a ring of lasting truth to them: "dedi-cated to the proposition that all men are created equal," "these dead shall not have died in vain," "government of the people, by the people, for the people." Then imagine reading this speech af-ter studying the history of the United States in the 1860s. The same words would take on an even greater depth of meaning.

In the same way, our study of Daniel will be enriching if we make the effort to understand the times in which Daniel and his friends lived. In those days the tiny nation of Judah, which had long been disobedient to God, found itself under attack by a new world power.

A Nation Under Siege

Back in the year 609 B.C., about 113 years after the northern kingdom of Israel was taken captive and exiled by Assyria (2 Kings 17), King Jehoiakim ascended to the throne of the southern kingdom of Judah. His immediate predecessor, his half-brother Jehoahaz, had served for only three months, in which "he did evil in the eyes of the LORD" (2 Kings 23:32). God allowed Pharaoh Neco of Egypt to take away Jehoahaz in chains; Neco also imposed an oppressive gold and silver tax on the people of Judah. The pharaoh then appointed Jehoahaz's half brother Eliakim (whose name meant "God has established") to be king of Judah, changing his name to Jehoiakim (meaning "*Yahweh* has established"; *Yahweh* ["the LORD"] was the name of God associated with God's covenant—see Ex. 3:15; 19:3-6). Although the meaning of this new name was essentially the same as before, the renaming was clearly a sign that Jehoiakim was now merely a vassal of the king of Egypt. This turn of events warned of the sure punishment that would come if the people refused to repent and obey "the LORD" (see Deut. 28-31; Jer. 7:1-29; 26:1-16).

After a short time, Jehoiakim's allegiance shifted not to the Lord but to Babylon, the latest threat to stability in the region. Then three years later, when Jehoiakim tried to realign with Egypt, Nebuchadnezzar of Babylon invaded Judah. This was the first of three Babylonian invasions, which took place in about 605, 597, and 586 B.C. The final invasion in 586 marked the destruction of Jerusalem and the end of the kingdom of Judah (2 Kings 25).

During the first invasion, "in the third year of the reign of Jehoiakim" (around 605 B.C.), a young man named Daniel was taken captive and deported to Babylon along with other young men "from the royal family and the nobility" of Judah (Dan. 1:1, 3). There he and his companions would be trained to serve in King Nebuchadnezzar's court.

Servants in Training

When they arrived in Babylon, Daniel and several other carefully selected young Israelite men were brought to Ashpenaz, chief of Nebuchadnezzar's court officials, to be trained in the language and literature of the Babylonians. Only the best would do for the king, so the qualifications for these servants in training were very strict:

- no physical defects
- handsome

9

- an aptitude for learning
- well informed
- quick to understand

And after three years of training, these young men would enter the king's service.

Like the vassal King Jehoiakim, Daniel and his companions also received new names, reminding them that they were no longer considered Israelites but citizens of their strange new land. Daniel, whose name meant "God is my judge," became Belteshazzar, which means "Bel, protect him" (Bel was a chief god of the Babylonians). Hananiah ("the Lord has been gracious") became Shadrach (possibly "under the command of Aku," the regional moon god). Mishael ("Who is like God?") became Meshach (possibly "Who is like Aku?"). And Azariah ("the LORD helps") became Abednego ("servant of Nego [Nebo, Nabu]," another Babylonian god).

The First Test

When the king assigned food and wine from his royal table for his new servants in training, Daniel resolved that he would continue to keep the dietary laws he had observed in Judah. Even though he was living in a Gentile palace, learning Gentile customs, and studying a Gentile language, he didn't have to eat Gentile food! The king's table would almost certainly have included foods that were unclean to a faithful Jew: pork, many kinds of seafood, and meat from which the blood had not been properly drained—to name just a few (see Lev. 7:22-27; 11:1-47). Daniel chose not to defile himself, not even when he was a thousand miles from home!

As our text tells us, God had already caused Ashpenaz, the king's chief of staff, "to show favor and sympathy to Daniel" (Dan. 1:9). Even so, the official was unwilling to risk going against the king's command. If Daniel and his friends became less healthy than the other young men after passing up the king's food—well, Ashpenaz's own life would be on the line!

Daniel was persistent, however, so he struck a deal with the guard who had been appointed to watch over them. For ten days he and his friends would eat nothing but vegetables and water, and then the guard could compare their condition to that of the other young men. Maybe this guard wasn't as quick thinking as Ashpenaz, or perhaps he figured he could enjoy more choice food for himself—but whatever the reason, he agreed to the test.

As the story shows, God honored Daniel's obedience, and after ten days Daniel and his friends appeared more fit and well-nourished than any of the other young men.

After Three Years

God honored Daniel and his friends not only with good health but also with wisdom and understanding. When their three years of training were completed, the young men from Judah were presented to the king and found to be without equal in the kingdom. God's gift of knowledge about every kind of literature and learning had made them "ten times" wiser than all the king's magicians and enchanters (1:20). As we will see later in our study, this ability did not go unnoticed by these other counselors to the king.

Additional Notes

1:2—Among the articles taken from the temple of God were some sacred goblets that play a major role in another part of Daniel's story, when Belshazzar orders them brought from the treasury for a royal banquet (5:2). These goblets were intended for making drink offerings in the worship of God (see Jer. 52:19), and when Belshazzar begins to use them to praise "gods of gold and silver, of bronze, iron, wood and stone," a hand appears and begins writing on the wall (Dan. 5:4-5).

1:3—Isaiah 39:6-7 adds a possible detail to this episode that the author of Daniel does not mention. Speaking to King Hezekiah, who reigned from 715 to 697 B.C., Isaiah declared, "The time will surely come when everything in your palace, and all that your fathers have stored up until this day, will be carried off to Babylon. Nothing will be left, says the LORD. And some of your descendants, your own flesh and blood who will be born to you, will be taken away, and they will become eunuchs in the palace of the king of Babylon."

1:4—Excavations in the region of ancient Babylonia (modern-day Iraq), which was also known as Shinar (Gen. 11:2), or the land of the Chaldeans (11:27-31), have uncovered thousands of complete and fragmentary tablets, letters, documents, and literary texts. The cuneiform script, adopted from the earlier Sumerian people of about 3000 B.C., included about six hundred signs and symbols—quite a challenge for Ashpenaz to teach to Daniel and his companions in three years!

1:5, 8, 12—Daniel's request for a vegetable-only diet probably had more to do with the way Babylonians prepared their meat than with an objection to meat in general. For faithful Jews, it was acceptable to eat several kinds of meat as long as it was properly drained of blood, a practice that Babylonians probably did not observe (see Lev. 7:22-27; 11:1-47).

GENERAL DISCUSSION

1. Why do you think God's Word contains so many passages that can best be described as history? Do you think people in general, and people who attend church in particular, are well versed in the history of God's people, both before and after the time of Jesus? What value is there in making the effort to learn more about this history?

2. Nebuchadnezzar laid siege to Jerusalem, finally destroying it in about 586 B.C. What are some ways in which people of faith are under siege from God's enemies today? Do we ever form allegiances with earthly powers instead of placing our trust in God? Explain.

3. Daniel and his companions were forcibly resettled into a new culture, where God chose to use their extraordinary faith as an example for future generations. Can you think of any contemporary examples of people whose lives have been severely disrupted? How can faith sustain us in such circumstances?

4. Daniel and his friends refused the royal food from the king's table. What does this incident teach us about the saying "When in Rome, do as the Romans do?" Can we learn anything about our own eating habits from this story? What's the most important point for us to learn here?

SMALL GROUP SESSION IDEAS

Opening (10 minutes)

After any necessary introductions, read Psalm 137 quietly (your leader should have extra Bibles available, if needed) and spend a few moments in silence reflecting on the emotions expressed by an anonymous psalmist in exile.

Prayer—Move from reflecting on Psalm 137 to expressing gratitude and praise, acknowledging that God is never far from us, no matter what "strange land" we may be in. Also remember people who, like Daniel, are facing new challenges of faith because of changed circumstances.

Share—Talk together about the emotions *you* experienced as you thought about Psalm 137. Were you surprised by them? Would you expect Daniel to express similar emotions as he wrote about his experiences in Babylon?

Focus—This lesson's dual emphasis is on the circumstances that brought Daniel and his companions to Babylon and their continuing obedience to God while living in exile. Throughout this time of study, be conscious of the many displaced persons around the world. Remember that someone doesn't have to literally move to another country to feel "exiled." Keep in mind also that God can use times of exile to develop extraordinary faith in people who continue to place their trust in the Lord.

Growing (35-40 minutes)

Read—Daniel is a wonderful book to read out loud, lending itself to dramatic emphasis and timely pauses. If any of you has a gift for expressive reading, perhaps you'd like to read Daniel 1 aloud. As a group, you could also read 2 Kings 23:36-24:7, an account of Nebuchadnezzar's first invasion of Judah (around 605 B.C.), during which Daniel and his friends were taken into exile.

Discuss—Use the following questions along with the General Discussion questions to think about how the stories of Daniel can affect our decision making in our daily living.

- Think about the people of the small nation of Judah, some insisting that their leaders must trust in God alone, others encouraging defensive alliances with other nations. Which side of the debate would you have taken? Explain. Can you think of any ways in which our leaders today face similar decisions?

- Have you ever felt "under siege" as you tried to serve God faithfully? How did you respond to the challenges you faced? Could your experience be a lesson for others? Explain.

- How do people typically react to God when their lives are disrupted? What do our reactions to difficult situations say about our faith?

- Daniel and his companions faced a difficult test of obedience when offered the king's bounty in their new land. What would be a comparable challenge for us, and how could Daniel's response inspire us as we serve God?

Goalsetting (5 minutes)
Look for examples of either displaced people or people "under siege" in the coming week. Note these examples or bring articles about them to the next study session. Focus especially on how God can use people of faith in these kinds of situations.

Closing (10 minutes)
Preparing for Prayer—Everyone is welcome to share joys and concerns, including items that have come to mind as a result of this study session. It can be upbuilding to mention answered prayers as well.

Prayer—Open your prayer with Psalm 137:4: "How can we sing the songs of the LORD while in a foreign land?" Acknowledge struggles and concerns, and remember together that because we trust in Jesus, all of this life is lived in the "foreign territory" of this world. Even so, we have much to be thankful for, especially the salvation that will bring us to live in God's presence forever. Pray for strength to live each day by faith while under siege by God's (and our) enemies.

Group Study Project (Optional)
Anyone who's interested may research one or more of the historical figures mentioned in Daniel: Nebuchadnezzar, Belshazzar, Cyrus, Darius, and so on. Or maybe someone would like to find or create a time line of events before, during, and after the exile and leading up to the time of Christ. Bible dictionaries and study Bibles can be helpful resources for this kind of study.

*Whose is
the greatest
kingdom
of all?*

2

DANIEL 2

Nebuchadnezzar's Colossal Dream

In a Nutshell
When Nebuchadnezzar makes an impossible request, demanding that his advisers tell him what he dreamed, only Daniel is able to tell the king both the dream and its meaning. In this story we are reminded that no mysteries are hidden from God, that even the greatest human empires are like dust in the wind, and that God's kingdom will never end. We also learn that faith in God leads us to God's truth.

Daniel 2
¹In the second year of his reign, Nebuchadnezzar had dreams; his mind was troubled and he could not sleep. ²So the king summoned the magicians, enchanters, sorcerers and astrologers to tell him what he had dreamed. When they came in and stood before the king, ³he said to them, "I have had a dream that troubles me and I want to know what it means."

⁴Then the astrologers answered the king in Aramaic, "O king, live forever! Tell your servants the dream, and we will interpret it."

⁵The king replied to the astrologers, "This is what I have firmly decided: If you do not tell me what my dream was and interpret it, I will have you cut into pieces and your houses turned into piles of rubble. ⁶But if you tell me the dream and explain it, you will receive from me gifts and rewards and great honor. So tell me the dream and interpret it for me."

⁷Once more they replied, "Let the king tell his servants the dream, and we will interpret it."

⁸Then the king answered, "I am certain that you are trying to gain time, because you realize that this is what I have firmly decided: ⁹If you do not tell me the dream, there is just one penalty for you. You have conspired to tell me misleading and wicked things, hoping the situation will change. So then, tell me the dream, and I will know that you can interpret it for me."

¹⁰The astrologers answered the king, "There is not a man on earth who can do what the king asks! No king, however great and mighty, has ever asked such a thing of any magician or enchanter or astrologer. ¹¹What the king asks is too difficult. No

15

one can reveal it to the king except the gods, and they do not live among men."

12This made the king so angry and furious that he ordered the execution of all the wise men of Babylon. 13So the decree was issued to put the wise men to death, and men were sent to look for Daniel and his friends to put them to death.

14When Arioch, the commander of the king's guard, had gone out to put to death the wise men of Babylon, Daniel spoke to him with wisdom and tact. 15He asked the king's officer, "Why did the king issue such a harsh decree?" Arioch then explained the matter to Daniel. 16At this, Daniel went in to the king and asked for time, so that he might interpret the dream for him.

17Then Daniel returned to his house and explained the matter to his friends Hananiah, Mishael and Azariah. 18He urged them to plead for mercy from the God of heaven concerning this mystery, so that he and his friends might not be executed with the rest of the wise men of Babylon. 19During the night the mystery was revealed to Daniel in a vision. Then Daniel praised the God of heaven 20and said:

"Praise be to the name of God for
ever and ever;
wisdom and power are his.
21He changes times and seasons;
he sets up kings and deposes
them.
He gives wisdom to the wise
and knowledge to the discerning.
22He reveals deep and hidden
things;
he knows what lies in darkness,
and light dwells with him.
23I thank and praise you, O God of
my fathers:
You have given me wisdom and
power,
you have made known to me what
we asked of you,
you have made known to us the
dream of the king."

24Then Daniel went to Arioch, whom the king had appointed to execute the wise men of Babylon, and said to him,

"Do not execute the wise men of Babylon. Take me to the king, and I will interpret his dream for him."

25Arioch took Daniel to the king at once and said, "I have found a man among the exiles from Judah who can tell the king what his dream means."

26The king asked Daniel (also called Belteshazzar), "Are you able to tell me what I saw in my dream and interpret it?"

27Daniel replied, "No wise man, enchanter, magician or diviner can explain to the king the mystery he has asked about, 28but there is a God in heaven who reveals mysteries. He has shown King Nebuchadnezzar what will happen in days to come. Your dream and the visions that passed through your mind as you lay on your bed are these:

29"As you were lying there, O king, your mind turned to things to come, and the revealer of mysteries showed you what is going to happen. 30As for me, this mystery has been revealed to me, not because I have greater wisdom than other living men, but so that you, O king, may know the interpretation and that you may understand what went through your mind.

31"You looked, O king, and there before you stood a large statue—an enormous, dazzling statue, awesome in appearance. 32The head of the statue was made of pure gold, its chest and arms of silver, its belly and thighs of bronze, 33its legs of iron, its feet partly of iron and partly of baked clay. 34While you were watching, a rock was cut out, but not by human hands. It struck the statue on its feet of iron and clay and smashed them. 35Then the iron, the clay, the bronze, the silver and the gold were broken to pieces at the same time and became like chaff on a threshing floor in the summer. The wind swept them away without leaving a trace. But the rock that struck the statue became a huge mountain and filled the whole earth.

36"This was the dream, and now we will interpret it to the king. 37You, O king, are the king of kings. The God of heaven has given you dominion and power and might and glory; 38in your hands he has placed mankind and the beasts of the field and the birds of the air. Wherever they live, he has made you ruler over them all. You are that head of gold.

39"After you, another kingdom will rise, inferior to yours. Next, a third kingdom, one of bronze, will rule over the whole earth. 40Finally, there will be a fourth kingdom, strong as iron—for iron breaks and smashes everything—and as iron breaks things to pieces, so it will crush and break all the others. 41Just as you saw that the feet and toes were partly of baked clay and partly of iron, so this will be a divided kingdom; yet it will have some of the strength of iron in it, even as you saw iron mixed with clay. 42As the toes were partly iron and partly clay, so this kingdom will be partly strong and partly brittle. 43And just as you saw the iron mixed with baked clay, so the people will be a mixture and will not remain united, any more than iron mixes with clay.

44"In the time of those kings, the God of heaven will set up a kingdom that will never be destroyed, nor will it be left to another people. It will crush all those kingdoms and bring them to an end, but it will itself endure forever. 45This is the meaning of the vision of the rock cut out of a mountain, but not by human hands—a rock that broke the iron, the bronze, the clay, the silver and the gold to pieces.

"The great God has shown the king what will take place in the future. The dream is true and the interpretation is trustworthy."

46Then King Nebuchadnezzar fell prostrate before Daniel and paid him honor and ordered that an offering and incense be presented to him. 47The king said to Daniel, "Surely your God is the God of gods and the Lord of kings and a revealer of mysteries, for you were able to reveal this mystery."

48Then the king placed Daniel in a high position and lavished many gifts on him. He made him ruler over the entire province of Babylon and placed him in charge of all its wise men. 49Moreover, at Daniel's request the king appointed Shadrach, Meshach and Abednego administrators over the province of Babylon, while Daniel himself remained at the royal court.

To Sleep, Perchance to Dream

Sometime during the second year of Nebuchadnezzar's reign—which meant that Daniel and his friends were probably still in training—the king began to suffer some restless nights. It may have been a recurring dream that troubled his sleep, and the king may have suspected it had a important meaning. Wanting to get to the bottom of this mystery—not to mention wanting to get some sleep—Nebuchadnezzar summoned his magicians, enchanters, sorcerers, and astrologers.

As soon as we read the first few verses of this episode, we begin to suspect that something different than a typical dream story is going to take place. Daniel 2:2 says that the king intended to ask his advisers to "tell him what he had dreamed." Certainly this must mean that he wanted them to tell the *meaning* of what he dreamed, right? But when we get to verse 5, it becomes clear that the king wanted his gang of wizards to tell him the dream itself!

Was Nebuchadnezzar suspicious of his royal advisers? Did he suspect that it was their habit to tell him only what he wanted to hear? If so, he wanted to hear the truth this time, and he determined that the only way to verify their truthfulness was to demand that they tell him the dream itself. Only then would he trust their interpretation of it.

The advisers quickly developed a strategy for responding to the king's outrageous demand: *Play dumb.* Acting as if they had not clearly heard or understood the king's request, they gently and confidently encouraged him to tell them the dream so that they could give its meaning. Only when threatened with death by a carving knife did they finally give the king an honest answer (perhaps their first ever): "There is not a man on earth who can do what the king asks! No king, however great and mighty, has ever asked such a thing of any magician or enchanter or astrologer. What the king asks is too difficult. No one can reveal it to the king except the gods, and they do not live among men" (Dan. 2:10-11).

They were so close to the truth! Not even the so-called supreme gods of the Babylonians could give the king his answer. But there was another, the only true God, who could.

Daniel as a New Joseph

For anyone familiar with the stories of the Israelite patriarchs—which would have included nearly all of Daniel's original readers—the opening of Nebuchadnezzar's dream account serves as an instant reminder of Joseph's experience in the house of Pharaoh (see Gen. 41:1-8). In that story, after retrieving Joseph from his dungeon, the Egyptian king told the young exile of his fitful dreams about seven fat cows and seven skinny cows, and about seven fat heads of grain and seven withered heads of grain. God revealed the true meaning of the dreams to Joseph: seven abundant years followed by seven years of famine. And when Joseph suggested that Pharaoh put someone in charge of storing grain so that people wouldn't starve during the lean years, Pharaoh immediately made Joseph his second-in-command over the entire land of Egypt (41:25-40). It's a rags-to-riches story that has inspired God's people up to the present day.

The book of Daniel too was written to inspire hope among people who were longing for signs of God's favor in difficult times. It's not hard to imagine smiles creeping across faces as people heard or read the first few lines about Nebuchadnezzar's dream and the hapless magicians of Babylon. Remembering Joseph, those readers and listeners would have caught the cue that Daniel was about to arrive on the scene.

Off with Their Heads
When the stymied seers told Nebuchadnezzar that his request was beyond human ability, the sleep-deprived king issued a decree that every wise man in Babylon be executed. Arioch, the commander of the king's guard, came looking for Daniel and his friends, intending to include them in the bloodbath.

Showing the same wisdom and tact that allowed him to avoid unclean food from the king's table, Daniel asked Arioch why the king had issued such a harsh decree. Then Daniel dared to approach the king personally and was granted a brief delay of execution (see Additional Notes for some thoughts on Daniel's relationship to the king and the time of these events). Returning to his companions, Daniel urged them to plead for God's mercy so that their lives might be spared.

An Enormous Statue
During the night, God revealed the mystery of Nebuchadnezzar's dream to Daniel. The prophet thanked God with an eloquent song of praise, acknowledging that only God's wisdom and power made it possible for anyone to know what Nebuchadnezzar had been dreaming. Daniel then sought out Arioch to say that the executions weren't necessary. Daniel could now give the king the answers he was seeking.

Arioch, who was apparently not one to pass up a chance to curry favor with his boss, told the king, "I have found a man among the exiles from Judah who can tell the king what his dream means" (Dan. 2:25). When the king asked if this were true, Daniel replied that it was not he who had discerned the dream and its meaning; the revelation came from the "God in heaven who reveals mysteries" (2:28; see Gen. 41:15-16).

Telling Nebuchadnezzar that the dream was about future events, Daniel described a colossus that the king had seen in his dream. The head of this "enormous, dazzling statue" (Dan. 2:31) was made of gold, the chest and arms were silver, the belly and thighs were bronze, the legs were iron, and the feet were partly iron and partly baked clay (2:32-33). As the king observed this statue in his dream, a rock was cut out of a mountain, "but not by human hands" (2:34). The rock struck the feet of the statue, smashing them and bringing down the entire colossus. Its crumbled pieces scattered like so much chaff before the wind. The rock, however, began to grow, becoming a huge mountain that filled the entire earth (2:34-35).

After telling the king these details, Daniel continued by telling the dream's meaning. Each type of metal in the statue represented a kingdom. Nebuchadnezzar's Babylonian Empire was the golden head—a description sure to please the king. His kingdom would be followed by a lesser one—probably the Medo-Persian Empire (539-331 B.C.), though Daniel didn't give it a name. A third kingdom would follow—probably the Greek Empire (331-146 B.C.), again unnamed by Daniel. And after that there would be a fourth kingdom—probably the Roman Empire (from 146 B.C. into the Christian era), also unnamed.

Then, during the reign of the fourth kingdom, "the God of heaven" would establish an everlasting empire—the rock that crushed all the previous kingdoms (2:44). From God's Word and from history we can see that Daniel's interpretation of the dream pointed to the coming of the Messiah, Jesus Christ, who would set up God's everlasting kingdom, the mountain that would grow to fill the entire earth.

A Confession Fit for a King

Nebuchadnezzar's reaction to Daniel's report might seem surprising to anyone not familiar with the earlier story of Joseph in Egypt. To those who remembered Joseph's promotion to second-in-command over all Egypt, Daniel's assignment as ruler over the entire province of Babylon would only seem fitting. Nebuchadnezzar himself, unknowingly of course, almost seemed to be trying to outdo Pharaoh. He fell prostrate before Daniel, honored him with offerings and incense, and lavished him with gifts. Most important, though, was Nebuchadnezzar's confession: "Surely your God is the God of gods and the Lord of kings and a revealer of mysteries, for you were able to reveal this mystery" (2:47).

Daniel didn't forget his companions in all of this, either. At his request, the king appointed Shadrach, Meshach, and Abednego to become "administrators over the province of Babylon" (2:49).

A Second Triumph of Faith

It was Daniel's trust in God that encouraged him to make the meal deal we read about in Daniel 1:8, 11-14, and his faith continued to serve well in this dream episode. Consider this: If Daniel had not been a person of faith, he might have agreed with the king's advisers that what the king was asking was impossible. If Daniel had not been a person of faith, he might have tried to hide or escape from Arioch instead of asking for time and then urging his friends to join him in praying for God's mercy. If Daniel had not been a person of faith, he might not have received the revelation of the king's dream, or in a panic, perhaps, he might have tried to alter the dream's meaning to make it more to the king's liking (for example, "You, O king, are that rock which will grow to be a giant mountain . . ."). But Daniel honored God with his unwavering faith, and God honored Daniel by providing the wisdom and the insight he needed to answer Nebuchadnezzar.

How about us? Is unwavering faith in God the foundation of our lives? Do we believe in God's ability to do what seems impossible? Are we willing to tell the truth exactly as we have received it from God's Word?

"Dare to be a Daniel" is a memorable song lyric many of us first heard when we were children. This dream incident—and nearly every subsequent event in the book of Daniel—teaches us what it means: *Placing our faith in God will never disappoint us.*

Additional Notes

2:1-2—The opening of this chapter tells us that Nebuchadnezzar's dreams took place in the second year of his reign. As noted earlier, this likely means that Daniel and his friends had not yet completed the three-year training regimen specified in Daniel 1:5. This would explain why Daniel and his friends, who at the end of the three years were considered "ten times better" than all the rest (1:20), were not yet included among the advisers summoned to tell the king his dream (2:2). At the same time, Daniel must have had some previous acquaintance with the king, or it seems unlikely that he would have been able to go to the king personally to ask for time to solve the mystery.

2:4—The phrase "in Aramaic" does not mean that the astrologers spoke Aramaic (which would have been highly unlikely). Rather, this seems to be a later addition in the text to indicate that in the middle of 2:4 the original language of Daniel switches from Hebrew to Aramaic. This continues through Daniel 7, at which point the language reverts to Hebrew. Aramaic was the language spoken in Palestine after the Babylonian captivity; it was also almost certainly the language spoken by Jesus and his disciples. While many attempts have been made to attach significance to this shift in language at Daniel 2:4, it most likely simply reflects the way this part of Daniel was first recorded in written form.

2:31-43—There is no universal agreement about the identity of the four kingdoms represented by Nebuchadnezzar's dream statue. An alternative to the interpretation given in the study notes is that the kingdoms are Babylon, the Median Empire, the Persian Empire, and the divided successors to Alexander the Great, the Ptolemies and the Seleucids (hence the feet partly of iron and partly of clay). Since Daniel himself refers to the Medes and the Persians as a combined empire (see 8:3, 20), however, it seems reasonable to follow the arrangement cited earlier (Babylon, Medo-Persia, Greece, Rome).

Note also that the descending portions of the statue reflect a decreasing change in value, not strength. While gold is more precious than iron, it certainly is not stronger. The last empire represented on the statue would be stronger than the others but would ultimately prove vulnerable because of its corrupt and divided nature.

GENERAL DISCUSSION

1. In the Scriptures, dreams often have significant meanings (consider the dreams of Jacob, Joseph, Solomon, and Joseph, the adoptive father of Jesus). Does God still speak through dreams today? Have we been neglecting an avenue of God's communication?

2. Nebuchadnezzar's wise men could not give him the answers he wanted. In what kinds of contemporary situations do people turn to "wise ones" or "experts" for answers when they should be turning to God and God's servants instead?

3. How important was prayer as Daniel sought an answer for the king?

4. Daniel told the king that the statue in his dream represented a succession of kingdoms. Wouldn't most despots be enraged to hear that their kingdoms would be superseded? What does it say about Nebuchadnezzar that he took this news so calmly?

5. Does it seem clear to you that the rock that was "cut out, but not by human hands" (Dan. 2:34), pointed to Jesus? Is the mountain that grew from this rock still growing in the world? Explain.

SMALL GROUP SESSION IDEAS

Opening (10 minutes)

Prayer—Consider together how Daniel and his companions must have felt as they spent the night in prayer, asking for God's mercy so that their lives would be spared. Then read Psalm 130 before spending a few moments in prayer, asking for God's wisdom and understanding in your study of this lesson.

Share—Mostly for fun, but possibly for insight as well, tell about a dream that you clearly remember. Or talk about different kinds of dreams people experience (some common themes include flying, falling, or being unprepared for an important event). Take care to be sensitive in commenting on what others share.

Focus—This lesson examines the mystery of Nebuchadnezzar's dream, Daniel's faithfulness in believing that God would reveal both the dream and its meaning, and an important prophecy about God's eternal kingdom. Keep this question in mind as you work through this lesson: *How can faith in God make me better able to help others learn about the one true God?*

Growing (35-40 minutes)

Read—You may wish to read Daniel 2 out loud together, or, because it's lengthy, you may wish to summarize the story together. Just make sure to cover all the important parts!

Discuss—Use the following questions to go deeper on various topics while working through the General Discussion questions.

- Who are today's volatile tyrants? Should we limit our thinking to the leaders of nations, or are there other tyrants who also control the course of people's lives? Explain.

- How do today's religious and spiritual leaders rank in the world's view regarding people who have the gift of wisdom? In your view?

- Nebuchadnezzar was told that his kingdom would be followed by several others. Will the "kingdoms" of the United States, Canada, and other democratic nations last forever? What role will spiritual wisdom play in their continued existence?

- The rock in Nebuchadnezzar's dream proved to be more powerful than any empire represented in the great statue. What are some of the little ways in which faith proves to be stronger than the world's greatest powers?

Goalsetting (5 minutes)
Discuss this possibility: Commit to praying daily for yourself and for everyone else in your group, specifically asking God to give each of you wisdom in your daily living. Then at the beginning of your next session you can tell about ways in which you've experienced God's answers to those prayers.

Closing (10 minutes)
Preparing for Prayer—If you're willing, share your thoughts on specific areas in your life in which you are seeking wisdom and discernment (see Goalsetting above). What "mysteries" would you like to see answered? You may also wish to mention particular praises or concerns you'd like others to pray about.

Prayer—Remembering Nebuchadnezzar's threats and Daniel's faithfulness, begin your closing prayer with a reading of Psalm 141. Then continue in prayer with specific requests that have been mentioned. Ask also that God's blessings of wisdom and faithfulness may become more and more a part of everyone's daily living.

Group Study Project (Optional)
The Bible contains many stories about dreams and dreamers. If you want to dig deeper into this subject, you may wish to compare one or two other dream stories with the one you've looked at in this lesson. Then perhaps you could report on your findings during another lesson that deals with a dream, such as lesson 4.

"The God we
serve is able
to save."

3

DANIEL 3

A Blaze of Glory

In a Nutshell

Daniel disappears from center stage briefly while his three friends show their faith by refusing to worship an image of gold. Their confidence and God's protection of them result in another confession of God's greatness by the king of Babylon. The friends also demonstrate the importance of not compromising on matters of faith.

Daniel 3

¹King Nebuchadnezzar made an image of gold, ninety feet high and nine feet wide, and set it up on the plain of Dura in the province of Babylon. ²He then summoned the satraps, prefects, governors, advisers, treasurers, judges, magistrates and all the other provincial officials to come to the dedication of the image he had set up. ³So the satraps, prefects, governors, advisers, treasurers, judges, magistrates and all the other provincial officials assembled for the dedication of the image that King Nebuchadnezzar had set up, and they stood before it.

⁴Then the herald loudly proclaimed, "This is what you are commanded to do, O peoples, nations and men of every language: ⁵As soon as you hear the sound of the horn, flute, zither, lyre, harp, pipes and all kinds of music, you must fall down and worship the image of gold that King Nebuchadnezzar has set up. ⁶Whoever does not fall down and worship will immediately be thrown into a blazing furnace."

⁷Therefore, as soon as they heard the sound of the horn, flute, zither, lyre, harp and all kinds of music, all the peoples, nations and men of every language fell down and worshiped the image of gold that King Nebuchadnezzar had set up.

⁸At this time some astrologers came forward and denounced the Jews. ⁹They said to King Nebuchadnezzar, "O king, live forever! ¹⁰You have issued a decree, O king, that everyone who hears the sound of the horn, flute, zither, lyre, harp, pipes and all kinds of music must fall down and worship the image of gold, ¹¹and that whoever does not fall down and worship will be thrown into a blazing furnace. ¹²But there are some Jews whom you have set over the affairs of the province of Babylon—Shadrach, Meshach and Abednego—who pay no attention to you, O king. They neither serve your gods nor worship the image of gold you have set up."

¹³Furious with rage, Nebuchadnezzar summoned Shadrach, Meshach and Abednego. So these men were brought before the king, ¹⁴and Nebuchadnezzar said

to them, "Is it true, Shadrach, Meshach and Abednego, that you do not serve my gods or worship the image of gold I have set up? 15Now when you hear the sound of the horn, flute, zither, lyre, harp, pipes and all kinds of music, if you are ready to fall down and worship the image I made, very good. But if you do not worship it, you will be thrown immediately into a blazing furnace. Then what god will be able to rescue you from my hand?"

16Shadrach, Meshach and Abednego replied to the king, "O Nebuchadnezzar, we do not need to defend ourselves before you in this matter. 17If we are thrown into the blazing furnace, the God we serve is able to save us from it, and he will rescue us from your hand, O king. 18But even if he does not, we want you to know, O king, that we will not serve your gods or worship the image of gold you have set up."

19Then Nebuchadnezzar was furious with Shadrach, Meshach and Abednego, and his attitude toward them changed. He ordered the furnace heated seven times hotter than usual 20and commanded some of the strongest soldiers in his army to tie up Shadrach, Meshach and Abednego and throw them into the blazing furnace. 21So these men, wearing their robes, trousers, turbans and other clothes, were bound and thrown into the blazing furnace. 22The king's command was so urgent and the furnace so hot that the flames of the fire killed the soldiers who took up Shadrach, Meshach and Abednego, 23and these three men, firmly tied, fell into the blazing furnace.

24Then King Nebuchadnezzar leaped to his feet in amazement and asked his advisers, "Weren't there three men that we tied up and threw into the fire?"

They replied, "Certainly, O king."

25He said, "Look! I see four men walking around in the fire, unbound and unharmed, and the fourth looks like a son of the gods."

26Nebuchadnezzar then approached the opening of the blazing furnace and shouted, "Shadrach, Meshach and Abednego, servants of the Most High God, come out! Come here!"

So Shadrach, Meshach and Abednego came out of the fire, 27and the satraps, prefects, governors and royal advisers crowded around them. They saw that the fire had not harmed their bodies, nor was a hair of their heads singed; their robes were not scorched, and there was no smell of fire on them.

28Then Nebuchadnezzar said, "Praise be to the God of Shadrach, Meshach and Abednego, who has sent his angel and rescued his servants! They trusted in him and defied the king's command and were willing to give up their lives rather than serve or worship any god except their own God. 29Therefore I decree that the people of any nation or language who say anything against the God of Shadrach, Meshach and Abednego be cut into pieces and their houses be turned into piles of rubble, for no other god can save in this way."

30Then the king promoted Shadrach, Meshach and Abednego in the province of Babylon.

A Hot Spot in Canada

Several years ago, an elder of the church I was serving in Ontario called to ask if I'd like to tour the cement factory he'd worked in for many years. Though I wondered at first if watching cement being made would be like watching paint dry, I accepted his offer. We agreed on an afternoon tour the following week.

I knew almost nothing about how cement is made (and don't remember many details from my visit), but the one thing I will never forget is that it involves a furnace. We began by walking past mountains of limestone and underneath long conveyors that took it into the processing area. Because of the machinery noise, we made a lot of hand gestures as we went along. Eventually we arrived at an enormous furnace.

This cement-making furnace was several stories tall, and it had small view-ports in its side panels to let people glimpse the hellacious fury inside. The heat, even many yards away, was nearly unbearable, and to say that the noise was like a constant roar hardly begins to describe it. It's impossible to imagine any living thing being able to survive the blaze inside. I'm sure I was told a technical name for this particular kind of kiln, but all I remember thinking at the time was that if I'd been Shadrach, Meshach, or Abednego facing this kind of fate, I probably would have said, "Point me to the nearest idol—I'm ready to bow down!"

Nebuchadnezzar's furnace was probably a bit more simply designed. If it was a typical beehive furnace, it would have had an opening on the top as well on the side for adding or removing whatever was being fired. Still, whether the furnace was for baking bricks or smelting ores, it would have held a fierce inferno—and for Daniel's friends the king commanded that it be heated seven times hotter than usual. It must have seemed that Shadrach, Meshach, and Abednego were headed for certain death.

It All Started with a Statue—Again

Maybe Nebuchadnezzar was inspired by the statue in his dream (Dan. 2), which represented the present and future empires. Or maybe he was just acting in line with the idol-worshiping Babylonian religious culture. Whatever his motivation, the king set up an enormous, golden idol—oddly proportioned at ninety feet tall and nine feet wide—"on the plain of Dura" (3:1). Then he demanded that all the "peoples, nations, and men of every language" (3:4) fall down and worship it.

Locating the statue on a plain would have made it visible as a gathering place from miles around. Since "Dura" appears to be a common name, based on *dur,* meaning "rampart," the precise location of "the plain of the rampart" is not known. If there was any particular significance to the location, it has been lost to history.

Also unknown is whether or not the statue was molded to look like Nebuchadnezzar. Convincing arguments can be made either way; the wording in Daniel 3:12, 14, and 18 can be taken to suggest that the statue bore either the image of a Babylonian god or the image of the king.

Calling All Officials

Daniel's absence from this story is hard to explain. Although he was appointed ruler over the entire province of Babylon (2:48), no reason is offered for why he would not have been required to attend the dedication ceremony for Nebuchadnezzar's statue. Later Daniel had his own opportunity to refuse to bow down to a pagan deity (see 6:6-12), but his failure to appear on the plain of Dura remains a mystery.

Everyone else in a position of authority was there: "satraps, prefects, governors, advisers, treasurers, judges, magistrates and all the other provincial officials" (3:2-3). The repetition of these titles, along with the repetition of several other lists in this passage (cataloging musical instruments, the various people who bowed down, and the names of Daniel's companions) serves as a wonderful literary device. Not only is this technique an effective memory tool for oral recitation, but the author also uses it to build suspense as we become increasingly certain that a conflict is coming.

It should be noted, in fact, that this chapter uses many devices common to ancient stories about conflict with royalty. As in the accounts of Joseph and Esther, the main characters in these kinds of stories first move from a place of prosperity or comfort into a dangerous situation, often because of someone's schemes against them. Then, at a moment when they are in greatest danger, the heroes prove to be victorious (often miraculously). What's more, their virtues—or God's—are lauded; and in the end they are rewarded with a higher position than they had at the beginning of the story.

In other words, the many court officials mentioned in this chapter serve as dramatic foils to our three heroes. The faith of Shadrach, Meshach, and Abednego stands—literally!—in sharp contrast to the bowing backsides of the other officials in the kingdom.

Would It Kill You to Bow Down?

Once the officials were all assembled, the scene was ready: the giant statue had been set up, and the musicians were poised to sound their instruments. So the herald announced the king's decree: "As soon as you hear the sound of the horn, flute, zither, lyre, harp, pipes and all kinds of music, you must fall down and worship the image of gold that King Nebuchadnezzar has set up. Whoever does not fall down and worship will immediately be thrown into a blazing furnace" (3:5-6). It's worth noting that this was no idle threat (no pun intended). For example, in Jeremiah 29:22 the prophet says in a letter to some later exiles in Babylon, "The LORD treat you like [the false prophets] Zedekiah and Ahab, whom the king of Babylon burned in the fire."

When the music on the plain of Dura sounded, however, not everyone bowed down. "O king," some astrologers piped up, "there are some Jews whom you have set over the affairs of the province of Babylon—Shadrach, Meshach and Abednego—who pay no attention to you, O king. They neither serve your gods nor worship the image of gold you have set up" (Dan. 3:9, 12).

While it may not surprise us to read this (especially if we've heard the story many times before), we should observe that the narrator chooses not to give us any prior insight into what Shadrach, Meshach, or Abednego thought about the king's decree when it was announced. Unlike the story in Daniel 2 (which portrays Daniel and his friends spending a night in prayer, pleading for God's mercy) or the story in Daniel 6 (which shows Daniel deliberately praying to God in defiance of the king's command) the story here portrays the three friends apparently deciding on the spur of the moment not to bow down.

In response, Nebuchadnezzar was "furious" (3:13—the same word describes him in 2:12 after his wise men failed to tell him his dream). He summoned the three Jews who had remained standing and, surprisingly, gave them a second chance: "If you are ready to fall down and worship the image I made, very good. But if you do not worship it, you will be thrown immediately into a blazing furnace. Then what god will be able to rescue you from my hand?" (3:15). In Daniel 2:11 we noticed that the doomed wise men made a reference to a God they didn't know existed. And here we see the king himself inadvertently announcing a challenge to the God of the Jews.

Between the herald's announcement and the sounding of the instruments, Shadrach, Meshach, and Abednego (along with everyone else there) had apparently been forced quickly to make a decision about bowing down. Now they had a few moments to revisit their decision, but their response was the same, if not more pointed: "O Nebuchadnezzar, we do not need to defend ourselves before you in this matter. If we are thrown into the blazing furnace, the God we serve is able to save us from it, and he will rescue us from your hand, O king.

But even if he does not, we want you to know, O king, that we will not serve your gods or worship the image of gold you have set up" (3:16-18).

The last part of their statement has been the cause of much discussion. Were these Jews expressing their fear that God might not choose to save them? Or were they making an extraordinary statement of faith in God similar to that of the prophet Habakkuk, who had written, "Though the fig tree does not bud and there are no grapes on the vines, though the olive crop fails and the fields produce no food, though there are no sheep in the pen and no cattle in the stalls, yet I will rejoice in the LORD, I will be joyful in God my Savior" (Hab. 3:17-18)?

A Hot Spot in Babylon

Furious again, Nebuchadnezzar ordered his furnace heated seven times hotter than usual. The king's strongest soldiers tied up the three Jews, and we can almost hear the original listeners groaning as the author uses one more list ("robes, trousers, turbans and other clothes"—3:21) to forestall the climax of the story.

The superheated furnace was so hot that the soldiers were instantly killed (3:22). But the three who "fell into the blazing furnace" (3:23) . . . became four! Nebuchadnezzar saw "four men walking around in the fire, unbound and unharmed," and he described the fourth as one who looked like "a son of the gods" (3:25). Although some commentators have suggested that this wording refers to a preincarnate appearance of Jesus, it could just as easily refer to an angel (see 3:28; note also the appearance of an angel while Daniel was in the lions' den—6:22). The king then called Shadrach, Meshach, and Abednego out of the furnace, praising their God as he did so (3:26). Not only were they unharmed and their clothing unscorched; they didn't even smell of fire (3:27).

At this point Nebuchadnezzar had another of his "moments of clarity." He praised God again, much as he had done after Daniel had interpreted his dream—but in a despotic kind of way: anyone who said anything against the God of Shadrach, Meshach, and Abednego would be "cut into pieces" and their houses would be "turned into piles of rubble" (3:29). For "no other god," he said, "can save this way" (3:29).

It was a step in the right direction, but God wasn't through with Nebuchadnezzar yet.

Additional Notes

3:1—One of the seven wonders of the ancient world was the Colossus of Rhodes, a statue of the Greek god Helios (Apollo) built around 280 B.C. of bronze and iron (for strength) to stand more than a hundred feet tall. In comparison, Nebuchadnezzar's oddly dimensioned nine-by-ninety-foot statue was probably made not of solid gold but of a wood frame with gold overlay.

3:2—"Satraps, prefects, governors . . ." This listing of various officials is typical of the kind of detail found in many inscriptions and on monuments from the Babylonian period. Each functionary had different responsibilities in the administration of the kingdom (compare to senators, representatives, governors, mayors, and so on of today).

The word translated as "dedication" is the Aramaic word *hanukkah,* well known today as a reference to the Jewish festival commemorating the rededication of the temple in Jerusalem in 165 B.C.

3:5—"Horn, flute, zither . . ." Various translations of the Bible give different names for the instruments used, such as sackbut, bagpipes, trigon, and more (see KJV, ASV, RSV). Though well-informed guesses can be made as to the types of instruments that were common at the time, it's difficult to say exactly which instrument is indicated by each Aramaic name given in the text of Daniel.

3:28-29—The king's decree is similar to one issued by King Darius many years later, when Daniel's life was spared in the lions' den (6:26-27).

_____

GENERAL DISCUSSION

1. Nebuchadnezzar was apparently trying to unify a diverse kingdom around the worship of a new common god. Is religion an effective way to bring diverse groups of people together? What difference does it make if this happens by coercion or by choice?

2. Based on what we know from just the first three chapters of Daniel, why do you think Shadrach, Meshach, and Abednego refused to bow down?

3. Would this story's lesson about uncompromising faith have been any different if the three friends had died in the fire? Why or why not?

4. God's angels are messengers (our word *angel* comes from the Greek word *angelos,* meaning "messenger"). What message might the angel in the furnace have been bringing?

5. Nebuchadnezzar praised God again at the end of this story. He also threatened to kill anyone who said anything against the God of the Jews. Do you think the king believed his own words of praise? What might have been a better response than the threat he delivered?

SMALL GROUP SESSION IDEAS

Opening (10 minutes)

As a follow-up to the goalsetting exercise from session 2, some of you may have some interesting and surprising responses to the "prayer for wisdom" challenge. If not, though, keep praying for each other. God's timing is not always what we want or expect it to be.

Prayer—Read Habakkuk 3:17-18, noting the willingness of Habakkuk to place his unwavering trust in God, even if all the signs he hoped for did not come to pass. Pray together that this time of study will help all of you develop a faith that's strong enough to praise God even when things don't go the way you might want them to.

Share—If any of you studied dreams and dreamers as suggested in the optional study project at the end of session 2, you may wish to share what you've learned. Or you could have a general, but brief, discussion about compromise: *When is compromise a good thing? When is it wrong?*

Focus—Shadrach, Meshach, and Abednego were not willing to bow down to a false god—not even when their lives were on the line. Keep this question in mind as you discuss this lesson: *What are some ways in which I have compromised instead of standing up for my faith?*

Growing (35-40 minutes)

Read—Of all the stories in Daniel, this one has the clearest ties to oral tradition. Perhaps someone from the group could read the chapter expressively—with plenty of emphasis on the numerous lists and repetitions—while everyone else listens (rather than reading along).

Discuss—Use the following questions along with the General Discussion questions to help you think about uncompromising faith.

• Rather than giant statues, today's idols can be ideas, trends, personalities, lifestyles, material goods, addictions, and more. What are some of the specific idols that people are urged or maybe even forced to bow down to today? What is society's attitude toward people who refuse to bow down?

• Name a time when someone you know (or know of) stood up for his or her faith. What impression did it leave on you?

• The astrologers in the story were quick to point out that Shadrach, Meshach, and Abednego refused to bow down. Why do many people see strong faith as a threat? Is it easier to get along with people if we compromise instead of standing firm? Explain.

• Throughout history, people of faith have faced many kinds of persecution. Do we still face "fiery furnaces" today? If so, what are they? If not, what does that say about our faith?

Goalsetting (5 minutes)

Changing from compromise to unyielding commitment is not easy! Try setting a goal in the coming week to be watchful of times when you may be tempted to compromise your faith. You may even want to jot down a few notes about incidents that occur. Take note also of examples of people who are standing firm in their faith.

Closing (10 minutes)

Preparing for Prayer—Not everyone gets an angelic visitor when tempted to bow down to a false god—but God does send other messengers to give us strength. Take a few moments to reflect together on some of the ways God may send us strength and encouragement to stand up for our faith in our day-to-day living. Also mention praises and concerns you'd like the group to pray about.

Prayer—Pray for yourselves and others, asking specifically for the courage to stand up when everyone else is bowing down. Remember also to pray for specific concerns that have been raised during this study session. Close, if you like, by reading a praise passage about God's protection, such as Psalm 121 or 124, or by singing a doxology such as "Now Blessed Be the Lord Our God."

Group Study Project (Optional)
The persecution of believers in God is not merely a historical subject; it continues today. Some or all of you may be interested in gathering information about persecuted believers. It may be a real eye-opener to learn about the number of people who face "fiery furnaces" today.

*What could
produce such
a change in
the king?*

4

DANIEL 4

Pride and Punishment

In a Nutshell

Madness descends on prideful King Nebuchadnezzar as his education about the God of Israel continues (a prominent theme in the first few chapters of Daniel). As we observe the king in his humiliation and restoration, we are reminded that arrogant pride has no place in the life of anyone called to worship and serve God. We also learn that even the bitterest enemy of God's people can learn to sing God's praises.

Daniel 4

¹King Nebuchadnezzar,

To the peoples, nations and men of every language, who live in all the world:

May you prosper greatly!

²It is my pleasure to tell you about the miraculous signs and wonders that the Most High God has performed for me.

³How great are his signs,
  how mighty his wonders!
His kingdom is an eternal kingdom;
  his dominion endures from
    generation to generation.

⁴I, Nebuchadnezzar, was at home in my palace, contented and prosperous. ⁵I had a dream that made me afraid. As I was lying in my bed, the images and visions that passed through my mind terrified me. ⁶So I commanded that all the wise men of Babylon be brought before me to interpret the dream for me. ⁷When the magicians, enchanters, astrologers and diviners came, I told them the dream, but they could not interpret it for me. ⁸Finally, Daniel came into my presence and I told him the dream. (He is called Belteshazzar, after the name of my god, and the spirit of the holy gods is in him.)

⁹I said, "Belteshazzar, chief of the magicians, I know that the spirit of the holy gods is in you, and no mystery is too difficult for you. Here is my dream; interpret it for me. ¹⁰These are the visions I saw while lying in my bed: I looked, and there before me stood a tree in the middle of the land. Its height was enormous. ¹¹The tree grew large and strong and its top touched the sky; it was visible to the ends of the earth. ¹²Its leaves were beautiful, its fruit abundant, and on it was food for all. Under it the beasts of the field found shelter, and the birds of the air lived in its branches; from it every creature was fed.

¹³"In the visions I saw while lying in my bed, I looked, and there before me was a messenger, a holy one, coming down from heaven. ¹⁴He called in a loud voice: 'Cut down the tree and trim off its

branches; strip off its leaves and scatter its fruit. Let the animals flee from under it and the birds from its branches. 15But let the stump and its roots, bound with iron and bronze, remain in the ground, in the grass of the field.

" 'Let him be drenched with the dew of heaven, and let him live with the animals among the plants of the earth. 16Let his mind be changed from that of a man and let him be given the mind of an animal, till seven times pass by for him.

17" 'The decision is announced by messengers, the holy ones declare the verdict, so that the living may know that the Most High is sovereign over the kingdoms of men and gives them to anyone he wishes and sets over them the lowliest of men.' 18"This is the dream that I, King Nebuchadnezzar, had. Now, Belteshazzar, tell me what it means, for none of the wise men in my kingdom can interpret it for me. But you can, because the spirit of the holy gods is in you."

19Then Daniel (also called Belteshazzar) was greatly perplexed for a time, and his thoughts terrified him. So the king said, "Belteshazzar, do not let the dream or its meaning alarm you."

Belteshazzar answered, "My lord, if only the dream applied to your enemies and its meaning to your adversaries! 20The tree you saw, which grew large and strong, with its top touching the sky, visible to the whole earth, 21with beautiful leaves and abundant fruit, providing food for all, giving shelter to the beasts of the field, and having nesting places in its branches for the birds of the air—22you, O king, are that tree! You have become great and strong; your greatness has grown until it reaches the sky, and your dominion extends to distant parts of the earth.

23"You, O king, saw a messenger, a holy one, coming down from heaven and saying, 'Cut down the tree and destroy it, but leave the stump, bound with iron and bronze, in the grass of the field, while its roots remain in the ground. Let him be drenched with the dew of heaven; let him live like the wild animals, until seven times pass by for him.'

24"This is the interpretation, O king, and this is the decree the Most High has issued against my lord the king: 25You will be driven away from people and will live with the wild animals; you will eat grass like cattle and be drenched with the dew of heaven. Seven times will pass by for you until you acknowledge that the Most High is sovereign over the kingdoms of men and gives them to anyone he wishes. 26The command to leave the stump of the tree with its roots means that your kingdom will be restored to you when you acknowledge that Heaven rules. 27Therefore, O king, be pleased to accept my advice: Renounce your sins by doing what is right, and your wickedness by being kind to the oppressed. It may be that then your prosperity will continue."

28All this happened to King Nebuchadnezzar. 29Twelve months later, as the king was walking on the roof of the royal palace of Babylon, 30he said, "Is not this the great Babylon I have built as the royal residence, by my mighty power and for the glory of my majesty?"

31The words were still on his lips when a voice came from heaven, "This is what is decreed for you, King Nebuchadnezzar: Your royal authority has been taken from you. 32You will be driven away from people and will live with the wild animals; you will eat grass like cattle. Seven times will pass by for you until you acknowledge that the Most High is sovereign over the kingdoms of men and gives them to anyone he wishes."

33Immediately what had been said about Nebuchadnezzar was fulfilled. He was driven away from people and ate grass like cattle. His body was drenched with the dew of heaven until his hair grew like the feathers of an eagle and his nails like the claws of a bird.

34At the end of that time, I, Nebuchadnezzar, raised my eyes toward heaven, and my sanity was restored. Then I praised the Most High; I honored and glorified him who lives forever.

His dominion is an eternal dominion;
    his kingdom endures from

generation to generation.
^{35}All the peoples of the earth
    are regarded as nothing.
He does as he pleases
        with the powers of heaven
        and the peoples of the earth.
No one can hold back his hand
        or say to him: "What have you done?"

^{36}At the same time that my sanity was restored, my honor and splendor were re-turned to me for the glory of my kingdom. My advisers and nobles sought me out, and I was restored to my throne and became even greater than before. ^{37}Now I, Nebuchadnezzar, praise and exalt and glorify the King of heaven, because everything he does is right and all his ways are just. And those who walk in pride he is able to humble.

A Heart Transplant for the King

It hardly seems possible that the Nebuchadnezzar we meet in the opening verses of Daniel 4 is the same king whose furious rage sent Shadrach, Meshach, and Abednego for a walk in the fiery furnace. This king is auditioning for a spot in the Psalms; his song in 4:3 sounds almost as if it were written by King David. "Wow!" we might say. "Maybe the miracle at the furnace changed him. Maybe he really learned his lesson!"

As we keep reading, though, it quickly becomes clear that it wasn't the miracle in the furnace that changed the king. It was something far more personal, and it was something he became eager to share with us. In a vivid narrative in the king's own voice, we learn about a mysterious dream, a bovine madness, and a merciful restoration that gave the king of Babylon a new heart—a heart to praise God.

A Lot to Think About

The king's praise prologue certainly gives us a lot to think about (Dan. 4:1-3). Wasn't Nebuchadnezzar recently subjugating "peoples, nations and men of every language," ordering them to bow down to his giant idol, with a death threat for motivation (3:4-6)? How can he now address these same people, saying, "May you prosper greatly!" (4:1)?

What are we to make of the "miraculous signs and wonders" that Nebuchadnezzar says the Most High God performed for him (4:2)? What will they turn out to be?

And, perhaps most surprising of all, is the king of the great empire of Babylon truly acknowledging that a foreign God, the God of the Jews, will establish an even greater kingdom (4:3)? Whatever could have brought about this change?

Only God Can Make a Tree

Again a dream sets events in motion. A "contented and prosperous" king goes to sleep one night and wakes up "terrified"

(4:4-5). As in the dream story in Daniel 2, Nebuchadnezzar sends for his usual assortment of wise men, but this time he tells them his dream. We might wonder if perhaps they've learned their lesson about telling the king only what he wants to hear but, whatever the case, they cannot interpret the king's dream (4:7).

Enter Belteshazzar. We know him as Daniel, as 4:19 reminds us. Why isn't he the first wise man summoned? For one thing, it makes a better story this way, and the first half of Daniel is like a collector's edition of well-told stories. It's more likely, though, that Daniel, as "chief of the magicians" (4:9), was the wise man of last resort. In a big kingdom with many decisions to be made, it was probably only when the underlings were stumped that Daniel got the call.

Nebuchadnezzar clearly remembers Daniel, even though he has forgotten an important detail Daniel mentioned earlier. The king began, "Belteshazzar . . . I know that the spirit of the holy gods is in you, and no mystery is too difficult for you" (4:9). Actually, what Daniel had said in the previous dream incident was that "there is a God in heaven who reveals mysteries" (2:28).

Then the king begins to describe an enormous tree he has seen in his dream. The tree grows until it reaches the sky and is visible to the ends of the earth. It provides food and shelter for every living thing until a holy messenger from heaven appears and says, "Cut down the tree" (4:14). And after its fruit is scattered and the animals and the birds have fled, only the stump and roots are to remain, "bound by iron and bronze" (4:15).

At this point, the tree—reduced to a stump—is referred to as a person. For "seven times" (generally thought to mean seven years), this person is to be drenched with dew, live with animals, and even have the mind of an animal (4:15-16).

The dream concludes with messengers (now plural) declaring their verdict on this person "so that the living may know that the Most High is sovereign over the kingdoms of men and gives them to anyone he wishes and sets over them the lowliest of men" (4:17).

"You, O King, Are That Tree!"
The picture of a world-spanning tree as a symbol for a nation or kingdom is not unique to the book of Daniel. In Ezekiel 31:1-9, Assyria, the kingdom that had been in power before Babylon, is pictured in much the same way as Nebuchadnezzar is here. And in Ezekiel 17:22-24 another prophecy about a tree

depicts the kingdom of the promised Messiah. The Messiah himself uses the tree image in his parable of the kingdom of God as a mustard seed. "When it grows," says Jesus, "it is the largest of garden plants and becomes a tree, so that the birds of the air come and perch in its branches" (Matt. 13:31-32).

Though God reveals to Daniel that the tree in Nebuchadnezzar's dream represents the king himself, whose territory has spread "to distant parts of the earth" (Dan. 4:22), it most certainly is not this aspect of the vision that so terrifies Daniel (4:19). Encouraged by the king, who sees Daniel's alarm, Daniel informs the king that he, Nebuchadnezzar, is the tree and that he also is the one who will become like a wild animal until "seven times" have passed (4:22-23). The king's humiliation will last until he acknowledges that God Most High is sovereign over all human kingdoms. The fettered stump is actually a sign of hope: although Nebuchadnezzar himself will be bound by his madness, his kingdom will remain and be restored to him when he acknowledges the rule of heaven (4:24-26).

Once Daniel has interpreted the dream, he offers sage advice (and not just for the king): "Renounce your sins by doing what is right, and your wickedness by being kind to the oppressed. It may be that then your prosperity will continue" (4:27).

Madly Dining Alfresco

It seems as though Nebuchadnezzar is able to keep his "wickedness" in check for a year, because his prosperity continues unabated. But at the end of that year, as he is walking on the roof of his palace, the king gazes out over the mighty city of Babylon and congratulates himself on his achievements: "Is not this the great Babylon I have built as the royal residence, by my mighty power and for the glory of my majesty?" (4:30). This display of unfettered pride is the cue for the dream's fulfillment to begin. A voice from heaven speaks, telling the king his authority has been taken from him. And he is immediately driven from his people to live with the animals until he acknowledges that the Most High God is sovereign over the kingdoms of the world (4:31-34).

It's hard to know what faculties or powers of reasoning remained to the king during his sentence of madness. In 4:34 we read that at the end of the "seven times" he raises his eyes toward heaven and his sanity is restored. Whether he retained some self-awareness during his punishment or perhaps was endowed again with some self-awareness "at the end of that time" is probably debatable (4:34). We do know that it is God who restores the king and makes him "even greater than before" (4:36).

In a closing word, as if to make certain that both heaven and earth understand that *he* now understands, the king concludes, "Now I, Nebuchadnezzar, praise and exalt and glorify the King of heaven, because everything he does is right and all his ways are just. And those who walk in pride he is able to humble" (4:37).

A Contemporary Assessment

Oh, we might wonder, *if only God would always humble the proud and elevate the humble!* It's easy to think that way—until we accurately gauge the level of our own humility before God.

Do we acknowledge that God is sovereign over all human affairs—including every part of our own lives? Do we recognize that everything we have is from God's hands? Do we truly understand how quickly it could all change if God chose to humble us?

Which is more insane—to eat like an animal in the field, or to gorge ourselves on honor and praise that we don't deserve? Both are signs that something has gone wrong with our understanding of our place in God's creation. We are not supposed to be beasts; we are called to rule wisely over the beasts—as well as over the rest of God's creation (Gen. 1:28). In the same way, we are not to exalt ourselves but to recognize God's rule over our lives.

Foolish pride is an affront to God's honor; self-exaltation robs God of the glory God deserves. In mercy the Lord does not drive us out to the fields along with Nebuchadnezzar, but we may not forget the king's parting words: "Those who walk in pride he is able to humble" (Dan. 4:37).

Perhaps the next time you're driving in the country and you see a herd of cattle grazing in a field, you could quietly remind yourself, "There, but for the grace of God, go I."

Additional Notes

4:3, 34-35—The king's two songs of praise appear to borrow phrases from several psalms (see Ps. 115:3; 135:6; 145:13). It may be, as some scholars have suggested, that Daniel "assisted" the king in his choice of these familiar words in order to comfort the Jews of a later period who were living under persecution. Or could it be that Nebuchadnezzar had learned from his chief advisor a thing or two about the Hebrew Scriptures, large portions of which Daniel may well have known by heart?

4:13, 17, 23—The Aramaic word *iyr*, rendered here as "messenger" in the NIV, has often been translated as "watcher." These are the only occurrences of this term in Scripture. The description of these watchers or messengers in 4:17 suggests that they are part of God's heavenly council (see Ps. 89:6-7).

4:16, 23—It's likely that the early readers of Daniel's prophecy, especially those living under the harsh persecution of Antiochus IV Epiphanes in the second century B.C., would have been familiar with the prophecy of Jeremiah: "Now I will hand all your countries over to my servant Nebuchadnezzar king of Babylon; I will make even the wild animals subject to him" (Jer. 27:6). They would have appreciated both the irony and the justice of Nebuchadnezzar becoming like the wild beasts. It also would have assured the people that Antiochus too was under the authority of God.

4:32—There is no independent historical evidence of either insanity on the part of Nebuchadnezzar or of a seven-year interruption of his reign. Such afflictions, though, were not unknown. There is evidence of royal instability—along with a temporary absence from the throne—during the reign of Nabonidus, who ruled Babylon from 556-539 B.C. Nabonidus was the father of Belshazzar, who ruled as coregent with his father till Babylon was overtaken by the Medes and Persians (Dan. 5).

GENERAL DISCUSSION

1. Why do you think the writer of Daniel casts Nebuchadnezzar as the first-person narrator of most of this story? What impact does that have on the reader?

2. How many significant trees can you think of that are mentioned in the Bible? Try to come up with five or more examples. What are some of the ways in which the kingdom of God is like a world-spanning tree?

3. While walking on his palace roof, Nebuchadnezzar boasted about building the great city of Babylon. Do you think the king's boastful pride was enough of a reason for the punishment he received? Why or why not?

4. Daniel advised Nebuchadnezzar to renounce his sins "by doing what is right" so that he might continue to prosper. Is this consistent with what we learn about faith, works, and blessings in the rest of the Bible? Do we win favor with God by doing what is right? Explain.

5. What's significant about Nebuchadnezzar's becoming like a wild animal?

6. Do you think we will meet King Nebuchadnezzar in heaven?

SMALL GROUP SESSION IDEAS

Opening (10 minutes)
Prayer—Begin your prayer time by reading together Psalm 145:1-13a. Then continue in silent prayer, asking God to use this lesson to help you identify areas in your lives that may be affected by sinful pride.

Share—To begin thinking about this lesson on Nebuchadnezzar's humiliation and restoration, reflect on a humbling or embarrassing experience you've had, and consider sharing it. What did you learn from the experience?

Focus—This lesson's main emphasis is about honoring God by giving up our pride, repenting of our sin, and living for the Lord who loves us and never lets us go. Keep the following question in mind as this lesson unfolds: *In what ways has my pride prevented me from praising and serving God?*

Growing (35-40 minutes)

Read—Once again, you may want to read the Scripture for this lesson during your session time. Because Daniel 4 includes first-person narration (4:1-18, 34-37) and third-person narration (4:19-33), it could work well to have two people read the different parts.

Discuss—The following questions are intended to help us think personally about the dangerous reality of pride in our lives and how it affects the way we honor and serve God.

• What factors may have gone into making Nebuchadnezzar a prideful person? Which of these factors may be present in our own lives?

• Nebuchadnezzar called on Daniel to interpret God's messages for him. Does this still happen today? How can others help us discern what God is saying to us? Why is it that others can sometimes see God's messages more clearly than we can?

• How does God humble people today? Can you think of some widely known examples (consider people in government, business, religion, and so on). What effect do examples like these have on the general public?

• What do you think about the ending of Nebuchadnezzar's story, in which he receives greater power and prosperity than before? Can we expect that if we humble ourselves, God will give us greater blessings in our lives? Why or why not?

Goalsetting (5 minutes)

It's hard to recognize our own pride. Try setting a goal to look in a mirror each day and to ask God for the humility to see yourself as God sees you, as others see you, and as you should see yourself. With the rest of the group, also discuss other constructive ways in which we might identify pride in ourselves.

Closing (10 minutes)

Preparing for Prayer—No one wants to be humbled in the way Nebuchadnezzar was. Take a few moments to think silently about times when you deserved to be humbled but received mercy instead. You may also wish to share your experience with the group. Feel free also to mention other personal concerns and praises.

Prayer—Open your prayer time with a reading of Psalm 145:13b-21. Continue in prayer by thanking God for humbling experiences and for the mercy of forgiveness, salvation, and new life in Christ. Pray also for particular concerns and needs that have been mentioned.

Group Study Project (Optional)

Some or all of you may be interested in writing a song in the style of Hannah's prayer (1 Sam. 2:1-10) or Mary's song (Luke 1:46-55), both of which convey a strong and moving message about pride and humility. Or perhaps you could try paraphrasing one of these songs by using contemporary words and images.

*Who wants to
be weighed
and found
wanting?*

5

DANIEL 5

Heaven's Handwriting

In a Nutshell

When a disembodied hand appears and writes a cryptic message on the palace wall in Babylon, Daniel is again called in to solve a mystery. Though a different king is on the throne, the sin of pride remains the same, and God's message declares the end for Belshazzar and the Babylonian Empire.
The meaning for us today? Those who are determined to defy God may also find their days numbered.

Daniel 5

¹King Belshazzar gave a great banquet for a thousand of his nobles and drank wine with them. ²While Belshazzar was drinking his wine, he gave orders to bring in the gold and silver goblets that Nebuchadnezzar his father had taken from the temple in Jerusalem, so that the king and his nobles, his wives and his concubines might drink from them. ³So they brought in the gold goblets that had been taken from the temple of God in Jerusalem, and the king and his nobles, his wives and his concubines drank from them. ⁴As they drank the wine, they praised the gods of gold and silver, of bronze, iron, wood and stone.

⁵Suddenly the fingers of a human hand appeared and wrote on the plaster of the wall, near the lampstand in the royal palace. The king watched the hand as it wrote. ⁶His face turned pale and he was so frightened that his knees knocked together and his legs gave way.

⁷The king called out for the enchanters, astrologers and diviners to be brought and said to these wise men of Babylon, "Whoever reads this writing and tells me what it means will be clothed in purple and have a gold chain placed around his neck, and he will be made the third highest ruler in the kingdom."

⁸Then all the king's wise men came in, but they could not read the writing or tell the king what it meant. ⁹So King Belshazzar became even more terrified and his face grew more pale. His nobles were baffled.

¹⁰The queen, hearing the voices of the king and his nobles, came into the banquet hall. "O king, live forever!" she said. "Don't be alarmed! Don't look so pale! ¹¹There is a man in your kingdom who has the spirit of the holy gods in him. In the time of your father he was found to have insight and intelligence and wisdom like that of the gods. King Nebuchadnezzar your father—your father the king, I say—appointed him chief of the magicians,

45

enchanters, astrologers and diviners. [12]This man Daniel, whom the king called Belteshazzar, was found to have a keen mind and knowledge and understanding, and also the ability to interpret dreams, explain riddles and solve difficult problems. Call for Daniel, and he will tell you what the writing means."

[13]So Daniel was brought before the king, and the king said to him, "Are you Daniel, one of the exiles my father the king brought from Judah? [14]I have heard that the spirit of the gods is in you and that you have insight, intelligence and outstanding wisdom. [15]The wise men and enchanters were brought before me to read this writing and tell me what it means, but they could not explain it. [16]Now I have heard that you are able to give interpretations and to solve difficult problems. If you can read this writing and tell me what it means, you will be clothed in purple and have a gold chain placed around your neck, and you will be made the third highest ruler in the kingdom."

[17]Then Daniel answered the king, "You may keep your gifts for yourself and give your rewards to someone else. Nevertheless, I will read the writing for the king and tell him what it means.

[18]"O king, the Most High God gave your father Nebuchadnezzar sovereignty and greatness and glory and splendor. [19]Because of the high position he gave him, all the peoples and nations and men of every language dreaded and feared him. Those the king wanted to put to death, he put to death; those he wanted to spare, he spared; those he wanted to promote, he promoted; and those he wanted to humble, he humbled. [20]But when his heart became arrogant and hardened with pride, he was deposed from his royal throne and stripped of his glory. [21]He was driven away

from people and given the mind of an animal; he lived with the wild donkeys and ate grass like cattle; and his body was drenched with the dew of heaven, until he acknowledged that the Most High God is sovereign over the kingdoms of men and sets over them anyone he wishes.

[22]"But you his son, O Belshazzar, have not humbled yourself, though you knew all this. [23]Instead, you have set yourself up against the Lord of heaven. You had the goblets from his temple brought to you, and you and your nobles, your wives and your concubines drank wine from them. You praised the gods of silver and gold, of bronze, iron, wood and stone, which cannot see or hear or understand. But you did not honor the God who holds in his hand your life and all your ways. [24]Therefore he sent the hand that wrote the inscription.

[25]"This is the inscription that was written:

MENE, MENE, TEKEL, PARSIN

[26]"This is what these words mean:

Mene: God has numbered the days of your reign and brought it to an end.
[27]*Tekel:* You have been weighed on the scales and found wanting.
[28]*Peres:* Your kingdom is divided and given to the Medes and Persians."

[29]Then at Belshazzar's command, Daniel was clothed in purple, a gold chain was placed around his neck, and he was proclaimed the third highest ruler in the kingdom.

[30]That very night Belshazzar, king of the Babylonians, was slain, [31]and Darius the Mede took over the kingdom, at the age of sixty-two.

Historical Details

God's Word does not give us any specific information about the death of Nebuchadnezzar in 562 B.C., 43 years after he assumed the throne in Babylon from his father, Nabopolasser, who ruled from 626-605 B.C. Neither do we learn much about his immediate successors: Evil-Merodach, 562-560 B.C. (who receives a kind mention in 2 Kings 25:27-30); his brother-in-law, Neriglissar (560-556); his son, Labashi-Marduk, who reigned only briefly in 556; and Nabonidus, the last ruler of Babylon (556-539). Nabonidus's son, Belshazzar, was either coregent with his father or may have been regarded as acting king while his father traveled in Arabia.

In light of the general historical record, it seems best to read the words translated as "father" and "son" in Daniel 5:2, 22 as "ancestor" and "descendant," which are also acceptable translations of the Aramaic words *ab* and *bar*, respectively. For a similar understanding of the word "father," see numerous references in the books of Kings that say a deceased king "rested with his fathers" (for example, 1 Kings 11:43; 14:20; and so on).

As long as we are stating who's who in this story's cast of characters, it's also worth noting that the queen mentioned in Daniel 5:10 is probably the queen mother—who may even have been Nebuchadnezzar's widow or daughter and was now the wife (queen) of Nabonidus. Belshazzar's wives and concubines were already with him in the banquet hall (5:2), so this queen was most likely not married to Belshazzar.

Arrogant Choices

By now we have become familiar with the style and format of the conflict stories in Daniel. Though they follow a formula and can be somewhat predictable in their outcome, each new chapter proves to be a delightful page-turner.

The opening of Daniel 5 presents us with the puzzle of a new king. Will he turn out to be as self-aggrandizing as his ancestor, Nebuchadnezzar? Will he be "teachable," learning to praise the King of heaven, as Nebuchadnezzar eventually did?

With a skillful use of foreshadowing and suspense, the narrator gives us an early indication of the way this king will go. While hosting a banquet for a thousand of his nobles, Belshazzar orders his servants to bring in the gold and silver goblets that Nebuchadnezzar plundered from the temple of God in Jerusalem nearly seventy years earlier (see Dan. 1:2-3; Jer. 52:17-19). Apparently these sacred vessels had been safely stored in the Babylonian treasury since that time.

Though Nebuchadnezzar learned to respect the God of Israel, Belshazzar seems determined to thumb his nose at the Lord. Perhaps this young ruler has been lulled into a false sense of security by the apparent absence of the Jewish deity since the days of Nebuchadnezzar. Perhaps Belshazzar is eager to prove that he is greater than his ancestors, and thus dares to claim by this gesture that the God of the Jews cannot touch him. Or perhaps it's the effect of the wine. Whatever the reason, Belshazzar decides to exploit the sacred vessels that were "taken from the temple of God in Jerusalem" (Dan. 1:3) and to lift them in praise of "the gods of gold and silver, of bronze, iron, wood and stone" (5:4). To say that Belshazzar's actions are disrespectful hardly begins to describe his arrogance and defiance.

Divine Instant Messaging

As the king and his guests drink from the sacred vessels, a hand appears and begins to write on a well-lit section of the palace wall. The vivid description of the king's reaction sounds almost like a Hollywood scriptwriter's notes on how to show panic: Belshazzar's face turns pale and he is so frightened that his knees knock together and his legs give way (5:6).

Just as Nebuchadnezzar did when confronted with a mystery, Belshazzar calls in his cadre of wise men. He promises that whoever can interpret the message will be clothed in purple, have a gold chain placed around his neck, and become the third-highest ruler in the kingdom (possibly after Belshazzar and his father, Nabonidus). Again the wise men fail to live up to their lofty titles (especially the ones called "diviners"—5:7), causing the king to become "even more terrified" (5:9).

The Message Revealer

Hearing the commotion in the banquet hall, the queen mother enters, properly addressing the king first, of course—but with an ironic greeting (5:10). Seeing the king's terror, she tells him about Daniel, reciting his résumé and assuring Belshazzar that Daniel can interpret the mysterious handwriting. For some reason it seems Daniel has fallen out of favor as "chief of the magicians" (4:9). Perhaps another king placed his own favorites in positions of authority after the death of Nebuchadnezzar. (A later reference notes that Daniel was "about the king's business" in "the third year of King Belshazzar's reign," but he may not have been serving the king in person—8:1, 27.)

After summoning Daniel, verifying his identity, and acknowledging his reputation as an accomplished seer, the king makes the same promise to Daniel as he made to his other wise men—quite a generous offer to an exile from Judah, whose God he has been ridiculing! But Daniel wants neither gifts nor rewards, telling the king he can keep them or give them to someone else (5:17). This time Daniel shows no fear or hesitation about what he's about to reveal (compare his responses to Nebuchadnezzar in 2:16; 4:19).

Daniel begins with a brief review of what happened to Nebuchadnezzar—and this is worth noting closely. Observe that the prophet makes clear to Belshazzar that all of Nebuchadnezzar's attributes—his sovereignty, greatness, glory, and splendor—were gifts from God (5:18). It was God who placed Nebuchadnezzar in his high position, and therefore God who extended to him the authority to take life or spare it, and to promote people or humble them as he chose. Daniel leaves Belshazzar no room to doubt that all of Nebuchadnezzar's power came from God. (Of course, the same is still true of every earthly authority today.)

Daniel continues by saying that Nebuchadnezzar became arrogant, his heart hardened by pride. So God stripped him of his glory and drove him to live with the wild animals till he acknowledged "the Most High God" (5:21). And just in case Belshazzar hasn't quite gotten the point, Daniel makes it perfectly clear: "The Most High God is sovereign over the kingdoms of men and sets over them anyone he wishes" (5:21).

One can only imagine what's going through Belshazzar's mind at this point. If he's wondering whether he too will be driven to live with the animals—well, Daniel doesn't let him wonder for long. Belshazzar hears that in spite of knowing these things about Nebuchadnezzar, he has not humbled himself. Instead, he has set himself against the Lord of heaven, taking the sacred vessels from the temple in Jerusalem and using them to honor the human-made gods of Babylon, "which cannot see or hear or understand" (5:23). And even as Belshazzar and his guests have held those sacred goblets in their hands, so their lives are in God's hands—and God has sent a hand to write on the wall, "MENE, MENE, TEKEL, PARSIN."

Weights and Measures

Before we look at the meanings of the words in this message, it's important to note that written Aramaic, like Hebrew, depends on something called *vowel pointing*. Vowel points are small punctuation marks that indicate how a word is supposed to be read. Many words share the same base letters, and only the pointing distinguishes them from each other.

Most scholars agree that the interpretation of the mysterious inscription is derived from the various meanings of each root word based, in part, on different vowel points. So, for example, one way to read the words is as units of money in that time period: the *mina* (*mene, mena*), the *shekel* (*tekel*), and the *peres* (singular of *parsin,* referring to a *half-mina* or *half-shekel*). Another way of reading them is as three passive verbs: "numbered," "weighed," and "divided" (halved). The third word, rendered as "PARSIN" in 5:25 and as *"peres"* in 5:28, can also be read as a play on words referring to "Persia" (*paras*).

With each of these meanings in mind, Daniel interprets the message for Belshazzar. God has "numbered" the days of his reign and is bringing it to an end (5:26); the king has been "weighed on the scales and found wanting" (5:27—a *shekel* was worth only about a 50th of a *mina*); and the kingdom will be "divided and given to the Medes and Persians" (5:28).

Just Deserts
Despite Daniel's earlier refusal, Belshazzar rewards him with the robe, gold chain, and position of honor (5:29). (Is Belshazzar now trying to appease Daniel's God?) But none of these gestures does Belshazzar any good, for he is killed "that very night" as Darius the Mede takes over the once-proud kingdom of Babylon (5:30-31).

In the end God reveals an important truth—not only for Belshazzar and the people of Babylon but also for the people of Israel who will eventually find themselves living under the persecution of another tyrant, Antiochus IV Epiphanes: *All authority comes from God.* All sovereignty, honor, glory, and power derive from the one Lord of heaven who holds all men and women in his hands. To deny or defy that source of power is to invite a numbering of our days.

Belshazzar may have forgotten about Nebuchadnezzar's arrogance, but anyone who studies Daniel closely will learn well that arrogant pride has no place in the lives of those who wish to serve God.

Additional Notes
5:1—Belshazzar's banquet for a thousand nobles may remind us of a similar event hosted by King Xerxes of Persia during the time of the Medes and Persians (Esther 1:1-8). The Medo-Persian Empire began with the death of Belshazzar and the conquest of Babylon (Dan. 5:30-31).

5:6—"His face turned pale." A more literal translation here might read, "His brightness changed" (see also 5:9). The same Aramaic word (*ziyw*) is used to describe the "splendor" of Nebuchadnezzar in 4:36.

5:7, 16, 29—Although the promise to make the interpreter the "third highest ruler" may refer to Nabonidus and Belshazzar as the first and second highest rulers, the Aramaic word *talta* here could also be translated as "one of three," meaning that the person would become ruler of one-third of the kingdom. In 6:2 we see that Daniel receives that type of administrative assignment under Darius the Mede.

5:12—The ability to "solve difficult problems" can be more literally translated as being able to "loosen knots." The Aramaic word *serah* here is translated as "unbound" in 3:25 in reference to Daniel's friends walking around in the fiery furnace.

5:23—Daniel's droll observation that Belshazzar's human-made idols "cannot see or hear or understand" is similar to Moses' assessment in Deuteronomy 4:28 (see also Ps. 115:2-8; 135:15-18; Rev. 9:20).

GENERAL DISCUSSION

1. Why would Belshazzar order his servants to bring in the gold and silver goblets from the temple in Jerusalem?

2. Why do you think God sent a hand to write the mysterious message on the wall? For whom was it sent? What did the message accomplish, since Belshazzar's reign was coming to an end that very night?

3. If Daniel was a teenager when taken into exile, he may well have been more than eighty years old at the time of these events. Would that have made a difference in the way he responded to the king? Explain.

4. Daniel reminded Belshazzar of what had happened to his ancestor Nebuchadnezzar. How can the stories of people who have gone before us help us learn to trust in God?

5. Why couldn't the king's wise men figure out the meaning of the message on the wall? How did the words of the inscription spell out Belshazzar's fate? Do you think he doubted the accuracy of Daniel's interpretation?

SMALL GROUP SESSION IDEAS

Opening (10 minutes)

Prayer—Begin by reading Psalm 20. Thank God for sacred things and practices, reflecting on some of them specifically. Ask God to make this study session a time that's set apart to honor the Lord our God.

Share—This session reinforces some of the lessons about pride that surfaced in the previous session. As a group, make a list of words you could use to describe a proud person; then make a list of words to describe a humble person (if possible, write the lists on a chalkboard or newsprint). Reflect quietly and honestly on which traits describe you.

Focus—If the last session could be summarized by *hubris* (overweening pride), this one centers on *sacrilege* (prideful desecration of sacred things). Keep these questions in mind during this session: *What has God set apart as holy in my life, and why? How do I honor God when I keep those things holy?*

Growing (35-40 minutes)

Read—To read Daniel 5 together in your group, several of you could choose to read the various parts out loud: narrator, Belshazzar, the queen, and Daniel.

Discuss—Use the following questions to expand on the questions listed under General Discussion. Several of these look at the situation in Daniel 5 from a broader perspective.

- Though his age is not stated, we can be fairly certain that Belshazzar was a young man (his father, Nabonidus, was still living). How does our appreciation for sacred things change with age? What kinds of events occur in our lives to correct the impetuous and sometimes foolish decisions we make when we're young?

- If you could recommend that God send a hand to write on someone's wall today, whose wall would it be, and why? What would the message say? What might a message on your own wall say?

- Daniel paid no attention to the king's promised reward for discerning the message. How much do we allow the prospect of some benefit to affect the way we deal with God's Word? For example, how would we deal with a situation that might help us financially but that we also knew was against God's Word?

- Daniel's faith was unhesitating in this story. What are some ways in which we can become more secure in our faith?

Goalsetting (5 minutes)
Set a goal to take note of short, public slogans "written on the wall" all around us. For example, a shoe company says, "Just do it"; a soda company claims that its product is "the real thing." Bumper stickers are another source of public sentiments. In general, what do these messages encourage us to do? How many (proportionally) go against God's will for us?

Closing (10 minutes)
Preparing for Prayer—Think of three- or four-word prayer requests, as brief (and yet profound) as God's message for the king. Share these, perhaps writing them down. Make them the foundation of your closing prayer.

Prayer—Read Psalm 20:6-8 again. Acknowledge the holiness of God, and ask for the strength to keep sacred things holy. Also include the prayer requests you've shared.

Group Study Project (Optional)
In addition to the Goalsetting suggestion, you may wish to keep an eye out for other examples of sacrilege in our society. Where and when are sacred things that are devoted to God profaned?

*When should
we not obey
laws—and at
what cost?*

DANIEL 6

6

Into the Lions' Den

In a Nutshell

A martyr story, a miracle story, a prophecy of the resurrection—all have been suggested as legitimate ways to read the story about Daniel in the lions' den. In this final narrative in the book of Daniel, we find our hero, a servant of God, set against the servants of Darius the king, and we find God's law set against the irrevocable law of the Medes and Persians. This story, with its theme of deliverance, serves as a fitting transition to Daniel's prophecies in chapters 7-12 pointing to the complete future deliverance of God's people.

Daniel 6

¹It pleased Darius to appoint 120 satraps to rule throughout the kingdom, ²with three administrators over them, one of whom was Daniel. The satraps were made accountable to them so that the king might not suffer loss. ³Now Daniel so distinguished himself among the administrators and the satraps by his exceptional qualities that the king planned to set him over the whole kingdom. ⁴At this, the administrators and the satraps tried to find grounds for charges against Daniel in his conduct of government affairs, but they were unable to do so. They could find no corruption in him, because he was trustworthy and neither corrupt nor negligent. ⁵Finally these men said, "We will never find any basis for charges against this man Daniel unless it has something to do with the law of his God."

⁶So the administrators and the satraps went as a group to the king and said: "O King Darius, live forever! ⁷The royal administrators, prefects, satraps, advisers and governors have all agreed that the king should issue an edict and enforce the decree that anyone who prays to any god or man during the next thirty days, except to you, O king, shall be thrown into the lions' den. ⁸Now, O king, issue the decree and put it in writing so that it cannot be altered—in accordance with the laws of the Medes and Persians, which cannot be repealed." ⁹So King Darius put the decree in writing.

¹⁰Now when Daniel learned that the decree had been published, he went home to his upstairs room where the windows opened toward Jerusalem. Three times a day he got down on his knees and prayed, giving thanks to his God, just as he had done before. ¹¹Then these men went as a group and found Daniel praying and ask-

55

ing God for help. 12So they went to the king and spoke to him about his royal decree: "Did you not publish a decree that during the next thirty days anyone who prays to any god or man except to you, O king, would be thrown into the lions' den?"

The king answered, "The decree stands—in accordance with the laws of the Medes and Persians, which cannot be repealed."

13Then they said to the king, "Daniel, who is one of the exiles from Judah, pays no attention to you, O king, or to the decree you put in writing. He still prays three times a day." 14When the king heard this, he was greatly distressed; he was determined to rescue Daniel and made every effort until sundown to save him.

15Then the men went as a group to the king and said to him, "Remember, O king, that according to the law of the Medes and Persians no decree or edict that the king issues can be changed."

16So the king gave the order, and they brought Daniel and threw him into the lions' den. The king said to Daniel, "May your God, whom you serve continually, rescue you!"

17A stone was brought and placed over the mouth of the den, and the king sealed it with his own signet ring and with the rings of his nobles, so that Daniel's situation might not be changed. 18Then the king returned to his palace and spent the night without eating and without any entertainment being brought to him. And he could not sleep.

19At the first light of dawn, the king got up and hurried to the lions' den. 20When he came near the den, he called to Daniel in an anguished voice, "Daniel, servant of the living God, has your God, whom you serve continually, been able to rescue you from the lions?"

21Daniel answered, "O king, live forever! 22My God sent his angel, and he shut the mouths of the lions. They have not hurt me, because I was found innocent in his sight. Nor have I ever done any wrong before you, O king."

23The king was overjoyed and gave orders to lift Daniel out of the den. And when Daniel was lifted from the den, no wound was found on him, because he had trusted in his God.

24At the king's command, the men who had falsely accused Daniel were brought in and thrown into the lions' den, along with their wives and children. And before they reached the floor of the den, the lions overpowered them and crushed all their bones.

25Then King Darius wrote to all the peoples, nations and men of every language throughout the land:

"May you prosper greatly!

26"I issue a decree that in every part of my kingdom people must fear and reverence the God of Daniel.

"For he is the living God
    and he endures forever;
his kingdom will not be destroyed,
    his dominion will never end.
27He rescues and he saves;
    he performs signs and wonders
    in the heavens and on the earth.
He has rescued Daniel
    from the power of the lions."

28So Daniel prospered during the reign of Darius and the reign of Cyrus the Persian.

In Search of Darius

Historians are quick to note that there is no evidence of a king named Darius who took the Babylonian kingdom from Belshazzar in the sixth century B.C. Neither is this "Darius the Mede" (Dan. 5:31) to be confused with later kings named Darius who are mentioned in Ezra, Nehemiah, Haggai, and Zechariah. Those were clearly successors to King Cyrus the Persian (mentioned in 1:21 and 6:28; see also 10:1; 2 Chron. 36:22-23).

Several solutions to this problem are possible. For example, Darius the Mede may have been appointed by Cyrus to rule over the province of Babylon. Or Cyrus/Darius may have been the same person, as an alternate reading of Daniel 6:28 suggests. It may also be possible that the history recorded in ancient Middle Eastern texts and inscriptions is the history that Cyrus and his successors *wanted* recorded, as opposed to the true course of events (note the late 20th-century Soviet attempts to amend history for political purposes—hardly a modern invention).

Fortunately our understanding of this story does not depend on a precise identification of Darius. In this chapter, in which Daniel does not even speak until he emerges from the lions' den, the sequence of events is what conveys the message.

A Flawless Administrator
After the defeat of Belshazzar, Darius appointed 120 satraps to rule throughout the new Medo-Persian Empire. Over these he set three chief administrators, "one of whom was Daniel" (6:2).

As the writer of Daniel makes clear, Daniel excelled at administration—so much so that Darius considered making him ruler over the entire kingdom, thus fulfilling every potentate's dream: all the authority with none of the headaches.

But that sort of arrangement would have been a nightmare for the other administrators and the satraps. Note that 6:2 says Darius made the satraps accountable to the three administrators so that he "might not suffer loss." Apparently part of the responsibility of satraps and administrators was to make sure the king's treasury was well supplied. In other words, they collected tribute and taxes from the many peoples they governed. It doesn't require too great a leap to imagine that the satraps may have been skimming some of these proceeds for their own benefit. Since we can safely assume that Daniel passed along all the tribute from his territory honestly, it's not surprising that he soon proved to be the most effective and efficient of the king's administrators.

Hearing of the king's plan to promote Daniel, the other administrators and the satraps tried to find some flaw in Daniel's work, some evidence of corruption. But after looking carefully, they concluded they would never be able to bring any charge against Daniel, unless it had "something to do with the law of his God" (6:5). We can almost see the light bulbs blinking on over their heads as they discover a way to trap Daniel.

Warning: Don't Feed the Ego

"O King Darius, live forever!" the officials begin. By now in our reading of these conflict stories in Daniel, it's becoming apparent that this sort of phrase tends to signal something: in 2:4, it's ineptitude; in 3:9, it's insincerity; and in 5:10, it's imminent disaster. In this case it portends subterfuge. The officials here make an appeal to the king's ego, suggesting that he issue a decree saying that for the next thirty days, anyone caught praying to any god or man other than the king must be "thrown into the lions' den" (6:7). "Put it in writing," the officials insist, "so that it cannot be altered—in accordance with the laws of the Medes and Persians, which cannot be repealed" (6:8—see Additional Notes on this point later in these lesson).

So King Darius issues the decree—unwittingly, we might add, considering his reaction to what happens next. He apparently hasn't thought about Daniel, who, learning of the decree, returns to his home and prays toward Jerusalem three times a day, just as he has always done (6:10).

After the jealous officials watch him at prayer (our text points out that he prays by an open window—6:10), they run back to the king and, before telling him their news, ask him to confirm the decree he has issued (6:12). Still not thinking about Daniel, the king reaffirms the decree, leaving himself defenseless against a sixth-century B.C. version of "Gotcha!"

Striking Parallels

The officials immediately spring their trap, identifying their victim: "Daniel, who is one of the exiles from Judah, pays no attention to you, O king, or to the decree you put in writing. He still prays three times a day" (6:13). The king knows that the first part of the officials' charge is untrue; Daniel is his most faithful administrator. But if the second part is true, if Daniel has still been praying toward Jerusalem, he has defied the decree and will have to be thrown to the lions.

A "greatly distressed" king spends the rest of the day trying to figure out a way to rescue Daniel from this fate. Send him out of the country? Prove that he hasn't really been praying? Find a precedent in which a law of the Medes and Persians has been reversed? Whatever the king tries to think of to spare Daniel, he isn't successful, for as sunset approaches, the officials return en masse (safety in numbers?), to remind the king that his decree must be carried out (6:15).

As New Testament-era readers, we may have noticed by now that this story bears some resemblances to the gospel accounts of Jesus' death and resurrection. As Daniel is cast into the pit of lions, however, the parallels become striking and unmistakable:

- Both Daniel and Jesus are watched closely by enemies and then betrayed.

- Both are praying before their arrests.

- The ruling authority—King Darius, Pontius Pilate—tries to avoid handing down the sentence of death.

- Both Daniel and Jesus are placed in chambers closed with a stone.

- The stone is marked with a seal.

- At dawn someone hurries to the chamber/tomb.

- The person presumed dead reappears, alive and well.

The most important difference, of course, is that Jesus was truly dead when placed in the tomb, not merely "as good as dead," as Daniel is described. Yet Daniel's experience is a clear "type" of the experience Jesus had—a vivid example of "what was said in all the [Old Testament] Scriptures" pointing to Jesus as Messiah and Savior (Luke 24:27). Just as stories about Moses and the Exodus prepare us to learn about Jesus and the way to God's eternal promised land, so the story of Daniel in the lions' den prepares us to hear about the miracle of our Lord's resurrection.

An Inevitable Outcome

Even if we haven't heard this story before, we can guess, from the outcomes of the stories in Daniel 1-5, that somehow Daniel will be rescued. Sure enough, when the king arrives at the lions' den early in the morning, calling out for Daniel, asking if his God has been able to save him, Daniel responds, "O king, live forever!" (6:21—perhaps the first time this phrase is spoken with respect in the book of Daniel). Continuing, Daniel says, "My God sent his angel, and he shut the mouths of the lions. They have not hurt me, because I was found innocent in his sight. Nor have I ever done any wrong before you, O king" (6:22).

An overjoyed Darius orders Daniel lifted from the pit. In the same way that Shadrach, Meshach, and Abednego emerged from the fiery furnace without even a whiff of smoke on them, so Daniel is found to be unharmed, without so much as a scratch to show for his ordeal (6:23).

The same cannot be said of the officials who schemed against Daniel. Curiously the text says they had "falsely accused" the prophet (6:24). According to the letter of the law, they had not; Daniel had, in fact, prayed to God in violation of the king's decree. But their intent had been to deceive the king. So the irrevocable law of the Medes and Persians had been upheld—just as God's law is to be upheld—while those who had violated the spirit of the law were thrown to the lions.

A New Decree
Like Nebuchadnezzar before him, Darius praises "the God of Daniel" (Dan. 6:26). Then the king issues a new decree that in every part of the kingdom, Daniel's God is to be feared and revered. The king's song of praise foreshadows the prophecies in this book that are still to come—about the eternal kingdom of God and the rescue that only God can provide.

This brings us to the end of the most familiar stories in Daniel, but don't stop studying here! More dreams, more angels, and more mysteries are still to come. There's even a prophecy of an "Anointed One" in Jerusalem (9:25). Could this refer to the Messiah?

Additional Notes
6:8, 12, 15—There is scant independent evidence that the laws of the Medo-Persian Empire were more immutable than any other laws in antiquity. Yet this view is consistent in the Bible. Esther 1:19 says the laws of Persia and Media could not be "repealed," and Esther 8:8 adds another detail: "no document written in the king's name and sealed with his ring can be revoked." Notice, though, that in both Esther 8 and Daniel 6 a new edict is written to counter or overrule a previous one.

6:10—The practice of facing toward Jerusalem for prayer did not begin with Daniel. Solomon's prayer at the dedication of the temple makes mention of praying "toward this place" and "toward the city" God had chosen (1 Kings 8:35, 44). David makes a similar reference in Psalm 138:2.

6:18—Sleeplessness is a common feature in ancient conflict stories. In Daniel 2:1 Nebuchadnezzar can't sleep; in Esther 6:1 we read the same about Xerxes.

GENERAL DISCUSSION

1. In what ways does this chapter testify to Daniel's professional integrity? His personal integrity? To what extent should the two be related in a person's life?

2. The laws of the Medes and Persians could not "be repealed" (Dan. 6:8). Is this a good idea? What effect would this have on the writing of new laws today?

3. Was Daniel breaking the law when he prayed toward Jerusalem? Whose law? When he was released from the lions' den, he told the king that he had done no wrong before him. What did Daniel mean by that? Should Christians disregard laws they do not agree with? Explain.

4. In this story, which of the parallels with Jesus' death and resurrection strikes you most powerfully?

5. How does God's law triumph over human law in this story?

SMALL GROUP SESSION IDEAS

Opening (10 minutes)
Prayer—As you begin, read Psalm 124, which reminds us that we cannot stand up in our own strength against God's enemies. Thank God for always being with those who have faith in the Lord, and ask the Holy Spirit to use this study time as a tool to build your courage.

Share—Has anyone observed examples of sacrilege since the last session? If so, how did you react to it? Take a moment also to think about a connection between keeping things holy and having personal integrity. Remember Paul's words: "Don't you know that you yourselves are God's temple and that God's Spirit lives in you?" (1 Cor. 3:16).

Focus—Personal integrity is the key concept in this lesson. When Daniel, the flawless administrator, is forced to decide between continuing his practice of daily prayer or obeying the king's capricious new decree, he chooses to continue his commitment to God. Keep these questions in mind throughout the rest of this session: *What is the connection between my faith and my daily devotion to God? Do I hide it, or do I let my devotion show, regardless of the consequences?*

Growing (35-40 minutes)

Read—Again one person could read the Scripture for this lesson while others listen. You may also want to read or review portions of the lesson notes.

Discuss—The following questions are designed to help everyone bridge the gap between ancient Medo-Persia and the world of today. Use these questions wherever they fit best as you do the General Discussion questions.

- If you rated your personal integrity on a scale of 1 to 10, with 1 being low and 10 being perfect, what score would you give yourself? Would others give you a higher or lower score? Explain.

- What evidence in your life and actions could prove to others that you are a Christian?

- If you were traveling in a foreign country known to be hostile toward Christians, in what ways, if any, would your behavior change?

- King Darius felt trapped after his ego allowed him to be duped. When has your ego gotten you into trouble?

- How does trusting in God "shut the mouths of the lions"? Does living by faith mean we will never be wounded, physically or spiritually? Would the point of this story be any different if Daniel had been devoured by the lions?

Goalsetting (5 minutes)

Between this session and the next, look for different ways in which faith is revealed, both in your life and in the lives of others around you. Also make it a goal to thank someone—in person or by letter, phone, or e-mail—for letting his or her faith show. Be prepared to share about this experience at your next group meeting.

Closing (10 minutes)

Preparing for Prayer—The personal integrity of people who follow Jesus is critical to the way others perceive Christianity. Before praying, spend a few moments in silence, thinking about areas of personal integrity in which you need strengthening from God. You may wish to mention other concerns and praises as well.

Prayer—Begin your closing prayer time by reading Darius's decree in Daniel 6:26-27, changing the pronouns from third person to second person ("he" to "you"). Continue by thanking God for amazing signs and wonders in the life of Daniel and for rescuing us through Jesus Christ. Use a few moments of silence to talk with God about matters of integrity (either silently or aloud) and to mention other items. Then end your prayer for this session with a reading of Psalm 138.

Study Project (Optional)

The remaining chapters of Daniel are often referred to as *apocalyptic literature*. Look up this term in a Bible dictionary or encyclopedia before your next study session. You may also wish to make a brief presentation on apocalyptic literature at the beginning of the next session.

What can such strange dreams mean?

DANIEL 7-8

Beastly Visions

In a Nutshell

As we move into the second half of the book of Daniel, we encounter two visions about strange beasts. These visions reveal the unfolding course of events in both Daniel's era and in the future. What's more, the Bible's interpretation of the visions assures us not only of God's control over history but also of the ultimate victory of the Lord's eternal kingdom.

Daniel 7

¹In the first year of Belshazzar king of Babylon, Daniel had a dream, and visions passed through his mind as he was lying on his bed. He wrote down the substance of his dream.

²Daniel said: "In my vision at night I looked, and there before me were the four winds of heaven churning up the great sea. ³Four great beasts, each different from the others, came up out of the sea.

⁴"The first was like a lion, and it had the wings of an eagle. I watched until its wings were torn off and it was lifted from the ground so that it stood on two feet like a man, and the heart of a man was given to it.

⁵"And there before me was a second beast, which looked like a bear. It was raised up on one of its sides, and it had three ribs in its mouth between its teeth. It was told, 'Get up and eat your fill of flesh!'

⁶"After that, I looked, and there before me was another beast, one that looked like a leopard. And on its back it had four wings like those of a bird. This beast had four heads, and it was given authority to rule.

⁷"After that, in my vision at night I looked, and there before me was a fourth beast—terrifying and frightening and very powerful. It had large iron teeth; it crushed and devoured its victims and trampled underfoot whatever was left. It was different from all the former beasts, and it had ten horns.

⁸"While I was thinking about the horns, there before me was another horn, a little one, which came up among them; and three of the first horns were uprooted before it. This horn had eyes like the eyes of a man and a mouth that spoke boastfully.

⁹"As I looked,

"thrones were set in place,
    and the Ancient of Days took his seat.
His clothing was as white as snow;
    the hair of his head was white like wool.
His throne was flaming with fire,
    and its wheels were all ablaze.

65

¹⁰A river of fire was flowing,
    coming out from before him.
Thousands upon thousands
    attended him;
ten thousand times ten thousand
    stood before him.
The court was seated,
    and the books were opened.

¹¹"Then I continued to watch because of the boastful words the horn was speaking. I kept looking until the beast was slain and its body destroyed and thrown into the blazing fire. ¹²(The other beasts had been stripped of their authority, but were allowed to live for a period of time.)

¹³"In my vision at night I looked, and there before me was one like a son of man, coming with the clouds of heaven. He approached the Ancient of Days and was led into his presence. ¹⁴He was given authority, glory and sovereign power; all peoples, nations and men of every language worshiped him. His dominion is an everlasting dominion that will not pass away, and his kingdom is one that will never be destroyed.

¹⁵"I, Daniel, was troubled in spirit, and the visions that passed through my mind disturbed me. ¹⁶I approached one of those standing there and asked him the true meaning of all this.

"So he told me and gave me the interpretation of these things: ¹⁷'The four great beasts are four kingdoms that will rise from the earth. ¹⁸But the saints of the Most High will receive the kingdom and will possess it forever—yes, for ever and ever.'

¹⁹"Then I wanted to know the true meaning of the fourth beast, which was different from all the others and most terrifying, with its iron teeth and bronze claws—the beast that crushed and devoured its victims and trampled underfoot whatever was left. ²⁰I also wanted to know about the ten horns on its head and about the other horn that came up, before which three of them fell—the horn that looked more imposing than the others and that had eyes and a mouth that spoke boastfully. ²¹As I watched, this horn was waging war against the saints and defeating them, ²²until the Ancient of Days came and pronounced judgment in favor of the saints of the Most High, and the time came when they possessed the kingdom.

²³"He gave me this explanation: 'The fourth beast is a fourth kingdom that will appear on earth. It will be different from all the other kingdoms and will devour the whole earth, trampling it down and crushing it. ²⁴The ten horns are ten kings who will come from this kingdom. After them another king will arise, different from the earlier ones; he will subdue three kings. ²⁵He will speak against the Most High and oppress his saints and try to change the set times and the laws. The saints will be handed over to him for a time, times and half a time.

²⁶"'But the court will sit, and his power will be taken away and completely destroyed forever. ²⁷Then the sovereignty, power and greatness of the kingdoms under the whole heaven will be handed over to the saints, the people of the Most High. His kingdom will be an everlasting kingdom, and all rulers will worship and obey him.'

²⁸"This is the end of the matter. I, Daniel, was deeply troubled by my thoughts, and my face turned pale, but I kept the matter to myself."

Daniel 8

¹In the third year of King Belshazzar's reign, I, Daniel, had a vision, after the one that had already appeared to me. ²In my vision I saw myself in the citadel of Susa in the province of Elam; in the vision I was beside the Ulai Canal. ³I looked up, and there before me was a ram with two horns, standing beside the canal, and the horns were long. One of the horns was longer than the other but grew up later. ⁴I watched the ram as he charged toward the west and the north and the south. No animal could stand against him, and none could rescue from his power. He did as he pleased and became great.

⁵As I was thinking about this, suddenly a goat with a prominent horn between his

eyes came from the west, crossing the whole earth without touching the ground.

⁶He came toward the two-horned ram I had seen standing beside the canal and charged at him in great rage. ⁷I saw him attack the ram furiously, striking the ram and shattering his two horns. The ram was powerless to stand against him; the goat knocked him to the ground and trampled on him, and none could rescue the ram from his power. ⁸The goat became very great, but at the height of his power his large horn was broken off, and in its place four prominent horns grew up toward the four winds of heaven.

⁹Out of one of them came another horn, which started small but grew in power to the south and to the east and toward the Beautiful Land. ¹⁰It grew until it reached the host of the heavens, and it threw some of the starry host down to the earth and trampled on them. ¹¹It set itself up to be as great as the Prince of the host; it took away the daily sacrifice from him, and the place of his sanctuary was brought low. ¹²Because of rebellion, the host of the saints and the daily sacrifice were given over to it. It prospered in everything it did, and truth was thrown to the ground.

¹³Then I heard a holy one speaking, and another holy one said to him, "How long will it take for the vision to be fulfilled—the vision concerning the daily sacrifice, the rebellion that causes desolation, and the surrender of the sanctuary and of the host that will be trampled underfoot?"

¹⁴He said to me, "It will take 2,300 evenings and mornings; then the sanctuary will be reconsecrated."

¹⁵While I, Daniel, was watching the vision and trying to understand it, there before me stood one who looked like a man. ¹⁶And I heard a man's voice from the Ulai calling, "Gabriel, tell this man the meaning of the vision."

¹⁷As he came near the place where I was standing, I was terrified and fell prostrate. "Son of man," he said to me, "understand that the vision concerns the time of the end."

¹⁸While he was speaking to me, I was in a deep sleep, with my face to the ground. Then he touched me and raised me to my feet.

¹⁹He said: "I am going to tell you what will happen later in the time of wrath, because the vision concerns the appointed time of the end. ²⁰The two-horned ram that you saw represents the kings of Media and Persia. ²¹The shaggy goat is the king of Greece, and the large horn between his eyes is the first king. ²²The four horns that replaced the one that was broken off represent four kingdoms that will emerge from his nation but will not have the same power.

²³"In the latter part of their reign, when rebels have become completely wicked, a stern-faced king, a master of intrigue, will arise. ²⁴He will become very strong, but not by his own power. He will cause astounding devastation and will succeed in whatever he does. He will destroy the mighty men and the holy people. ²⁵He will cause deceit to prosper, and he will consider himself superior. When they feel secure, he will destroy many and take his stand against the Prince of princes. Yet he will be destroyed, but not by human power.

²⁶"The vision of the evenings and mornings that has been given you is true, but seal up the vision, for it concerns the distant future."

²⁷I, Daniel, was exhausted and lay ill for several days. Then I got up and went about the king's business. I was appalled by the vision; it was beyond understanding.

A Little More History

For the same reasons that some people decide they will never be able to understand the book of Revelation, it's easy to be intimidated by these vision accounts in the second half of Daniel. But if we take the time to learn a little more of the history of the intertestamental period, nearly all of the important pieces fall into place. Not only do we begin to see why Daniel's book was such a comfort to Jewish people living under persecution in the last few centuries before Christ, we also receive assurance about our own future.

In the first half of Daniel we witnessed the rise and fall of the Babylonian Empire. Darius the Mede ruled next in Babylon (Dan. 5:31), and after him came Cyrus the Persian (6:28)—or perhaps Darius ruled under Cyrus or they were even the same person (see text notes on 5:31 and 6:28 in the *NIV Study Bible*). These events in Daniel 1-6 covered the years from about 605-539 B.C.

In 538 B.C. King Cyrus issued his edict of restoration, allowing exiled Jews to return to Jerusalem. The Medo-Persian Empire itself continued for more than two centuries under a succession of kings, including some others named Darius (mentioned in Ezra and Nehemiah) and Xerxes (Xerxes I is also known by the Hebrew name *Ahasuerus* in the book of Esther). In 334 B.C. a young leader named Alexander of Macedon began redrawing the map of the world, establishing a Greek Empire (more appropriately, Macedonian). It's nearly impossible to overstate the hellenizing effects of Alexander the Great's conquests in every corner of his empire. The influence of Greek thought in philosophy, art, literature, science, and many other fields continues to this day.

Many battles for succession followed Alexander's death in 323 B.C., and the empire was eventually divided under four of his generals: Lysimachus, Antipater, Ptolemy, and Seleucus. Successors to the final two, the Ptolemies and Seleucids, fought repeatedly for control of Palestine. Most important for the purposes of our study is that one of the later Seleucid kings, coming to power in 175 B.C., was the notoriously oppressive Antiochus IV Epiphanes, probably the "small horn" of Daniel 8:9.

A Word About Principles of Interpretation

In addition to learning a bit of history, it's also important to know that people interpret these visions in several different ways. Some interpreters believe they apply only to historical events that took place between Daniel's day and the time of the Jewish persecution under Antiochus IV Epiphanes from 167-164 B.C. Many of these same interpreters believe the book of Daniel was not written until *after* these events had taken place; in other words, they regard it as prophecy written after the fact.

Another interpretation involves reading these passages as end-time prophecies to predict the precise sequence of events that will occur at the end of time. Supporting that view is the scene of final judgment in Daniel 7:9-10; opposed is the fact that the Bible's own interpretation of the vision in Daniel 8 refers specifically to events that took place during the intertestamental period.

In this study we take the "both/and" approach, based on a Reformed understanding that biblical prophecy speaks to the people of its day as well as to peoples of later times, with (usually partial) fulfillments possible not only within the era in which it's delivered but also at later times and ultimately at the end of time, when God's kingdom will be complete. In other words, the visions in the book of Daniel are prophecies revealed to Daniel for the comfort of Jewish people who would turn to them while living under persecution, but they can also serve to comfort people in every age who await the final judgment of God and the victory of God's kingdom.

Lions and Leopards and Bears—Oh, My!

At the beginning of the vision in Daniel 7, the prophet saw "the four winds of heaven churning up the great sea" (7:2). In ancient times the powerful, formidable seas were believed to be the source of evil (see Ps. 74:12-17; Isa. 27:1). Consider also the significance of Rev. 21:1: "Then I saw a new heaven and a new earth, for the first heaven and the first earth had passed away, *and there was no longer any sea.*" In Daniel's vision, the winds drew four great beasts out of the depths of the sea.

The first beast had the appearance of a winged lion, a symbol that archaeologists have often found among Babylonian ruins. In the vision, its wings were torn off, and it was made to stand "on two feet like a man," and it received the heart of a man (Dan. 7:4). This detail may be either a reference to the gradual stripping of power from the Babylonians by the Medes and Persians, or a reference to the humbling and rehumanizing of Nebuchadnezzar, who symbolized the entire empire. Or perhaps both interpretations apply, happening at different times.

The second beast was a bear, and although there is no archaeological evidence linking bears to the Medo-Persian Empire, the lopsided nature of the bear may well represent the Persian dominance in that alliance. The three ribs in the bear's mouth probably symbolize three major enemies whom the Medes and Persians defeated.

The leopard likely represents the Greek Empire. Its wings would signify the swiftness of Alexander's campaign to conquer the known world at that time, and the leopard's four heads correspond with the four generals who divided Alexander's kingdom after his death (compare 8:5, 21-22).

The fourth beast with its ten horns (signifying complete power) was so terrifying that it couldn't be compared to any familiar animal, and with its iron teeth it probably represents the Roman Empire, or perhaps the succession of later kings after Alexander (see 2:40-43; see also Additional Notes on 7:7).

While Daniel was considering the ten horns of this beast, a little horn emerged from among the others (7:8). In the next vision the emergence of a small horn (8:9-11, 23-25) clearly describes the rise to power of Antiochus IV Epiphanes, which may also be part of the meaning here. It's also possible that at this point the vision becomes a prophecy not only of Israel's future but also of the world's. In that case, we probably should view that little horn in the same way we view the "man of lawlessness" in 2 Thessalonians 2:3-4, the antichrists of 1 John 2:18-22, and the beasts of Revelation 13 and 19:19-20 (again, see Additional Notes). So Daniel shows us that one cruel king can be a type of person whom we will find again and again throughout history. "He will become very strong, but not by his own power. He will cause astounding devastation and will succeed in whatever he does. He will destroy the mighty men and the holy people. He will cause deceit to prosper, and he will consider himself superior" (Dan. 8:24-25). Doesn't that sound like many rulers who have risen and fallen in history?

Daniel 7:9-10 describes a scene of final judgment remarkably similar to scenes we find in Revelation 5 and 19-20, while the appearance of "one like a son of man, coming with the clouds of heaven" (Dan. 7:13) is as clear a reference to the Messiah as we are likely to find in any Old Testament prophecy (see Matt. 24:30-31; 26:62-64).

More Beasts, More Horns

In the vision recorded in Daniel 8, Daniel saw himself at the king's citadel in Susa, a major city on the trade routes east of Babylon. Archaeologists have unearthed much of this ancient city, including the palace, which is also mentioned in the book of Esther (see Esther 1:2; 2:3).

In this vision Daniel first saw a powerful two-horned ram, followed by a goat with a single prominent horn. Although the ram had been crashing about, doing whatever it pleased (Dan.

8:4), it met its match in the goat. The goat knocked the ram to the ground and trampled it, continuing to grow in power until suddenly its single horn was broken off and replaced by four horns growing up "toward the four winds of heaven" (8:8). Again a small horn emerged. It extended its power as far as "the Beautiful Land" (8:9—a reference to Palestine), reached as high as the starry host (8:10—again see Additional Notes), and "set itself up to be as great as the Prince of the host," even taking over "the daily sacrifice" (8:11-12).

At this point Daniel heard the voices of two "holy ones," one asking the other how long it would be until the vision was fulfilled (8:13). Addressing Daniel, one of them said it would be 2,300 evenings and mornings (when the sacrifices were offered) until the sanctuary would be reconsecrated (8:14).

The Best Interpretation

We often find that the Bible is its own best interpreter. This is especially true when trying to understand texts like these.

In Daniel 7-8 the Bible's own interpretations are conveniently included along with the visions there. In the second half of chapter 7 we learn that Daniel's dream of four beasts was about four kingdoms (probably the same as in the dream of the statue in Dan. 2). And in the second half of chapter 8 we read of the angel Gabriel telling Daniel that the ram and the goat represent the kings of Medo-Persia and of Greece. In addition to describing these future events, Daniel's heavenly interpreters also gave him a glimpse of the Lord's ultimate plan— to establish God's own eternal kingdom through "one like a son of man" (7:13), or "the Prince of princes" (8:25). "His kingdom will be an everlasting kingdom, and all rulers will worship and obey him," according to the interpreter in 7:27 (see 2:44-45).

Waiting with Confidence

Even though Daniel himself was troubled by these two visions, they must have provided strong comfort to the people who turned to them centuries later. When the worst of the oppression began under Antiochus IV Epiphanes in 168-164 B.C., the people could trust that it would not last forever. When that brutal tyrant stood in the temple, ordered an end to the daily sacrifices, and declared himself equal to God (see Additional Notes), the people knew that the sanctuary of the Lord would one day be restored and reconsecrated (8:14).

That same comfort can be ours as we see kingdoms rise and fall throughout the world in our own day. In all times and places the affairs of humanity are in the hands of God, and in the end God's judgment will set all things right (7:26-27).

Additional Notes

7:7—Different commentators give different identities to the fourth beast. If the bear and the leopard are understood to represent the Medes and the Persians separately, then the fourth beast would be the Greek Empire, out of which emerged Antiochus IV Epiphanes, who is often recognized as represented by the small horn. The second vision, however, clearly states that the two-horned ram represented "the kings of Media and Persia" together (8:20), making it more likely that the bear in the first vision is also Medo-Persia. If so, the fourth beast represents either the Roman Empire or the succession of kings that followed Alexander the Great.

It is often impossible to identify precisely what certain symbols and pictures in biblical dreams and visions refer to, especially since they can have multiple interpretations at different levels and at different times. In this study we want to recognize that while we can make some educated guesses with the help of clues from history and from the Bible itself, we also have to step back and recognize that (1) we most likely will not understand every detail (this type of literature isn't intended for precise, scientific interpretation anyway) and (2) the prevailing, underlying message in all of these pictures is that human kingdoms will rise and fall (under God's sovereign control) but God's kingdom is forever.

8:2—The modern city of Shushan in southwestern Iran sits on the site of ancient Susa. A small tower located on a side of the ancient palace hill reportedly marks the burial site of the prophet Daniel.

8:9-12, 23-25—Although the book of Daniel does not refer specifically to Antiochus IV Epiphanes, a Seleucid king who reigned from 175-164 B.C., the apocryphal book of 1 Maccabees (1:10) helps us identify this tyrant as a likely representation of the small horn in Daniel's vision of the ram and goat. (See also text notes on Dan. 8:9-12 in the *NIV Study Bible*.) In connection with the small horn mentioned in 7:8, 24-25, this boastful, arrogant leader is also similar to antichrists described in 2 Thessalonians 2:1-12 and in Revelation 13 and 19. It is certainly possible that the small horn is intended to symbolize *both* Antiochus and future antichrists. As the apostle John puts it, "Many antichrists have come" (1 John 2:18), and "many deceivers, who do not acknowledge Jesus Christ as coming in the flesh, have gone out into the world. Any such person is the deceiver and the antichrist" (2 John 7).

The little horn's influence on "the starry host" (8:10) may also remind us of similar passages in Revelation that describe a portion of the stars being darkened or thrown to the earth (see Rev. 6:13; 8:12; 12:4).

8:14—Numbers in apocalyptic texts can often be puzzling. The "2,300 evenings and mornings" should probably be understood as about three and a half years of evening and morning sacrifices, which would take place over 1,150 days. (See also "time, times and half a time"—7:25.) These figures coincide with the length of the persecution during the last few years of Antiochus's reign, and they may also symbolize the limited period in which God's people will suffer severe persecution at the end of time (see Rev. 11:2-3).

GENERAL DISCUSSION

1. Instead of sending Daniel visions of a lion, a bear, a leopard, a ten-horned beast, a ram, and a goat, why didn't God just tell him plainly about the Medes, Persians, Greeks, and so on? What purposes might the animal symbols serve?

2. What relationship is there between the stories of faith in the first half of Daniel and the beastly visions in Daniel 7-8? What role does faith play in the vision accounts?

3. Try to picture yourself as a Jew living under persecution sometime after the return from exile (538 B.C.) and before the coming of Christ. How do you think you would have reacted to these vision stories in the book of Daniel? Would you have believed what they said about the end of persecution and the restoration of the temple? Why or why not?

4. Antiochus was a type of antichrist living before Christ was even born. Who are some of the people most strongly opposed to the reign of Christ today? How do they oppress believers? What do Daniel's visions say about the destiny of such oppressors?

5. How can we use these prophecies in God's Word to encourage believers and strengthen faith today?

SMALL GROUP SESSION IDEAS

Opening (10 minutes)
Prayer—Since these chapters of Daniel are closely related to Revelation, you could begin your opening prayer with words of praise from Revelation 4:8, 11. (You could also sing the words of these passages, familiar to many Christians in popular hymns and praise songs.) Then continue by asking God for eyes of faith to see clearly the meaning of the visions in Daniel 7-8.

Share—One of the goals suggested in session 6 was to compliment someone who allowed his or her faith to show. If you followed through on this suggestion, share how it felt to be an encourager. You also could take a moment to think about this question together: *Why don't we encourage people this way more often?*

Focus—Daniel's visions of future kingdoms may seem far removed from our daily work, play, church, and family life. Keep in mind that the ultimate message—not just in Daniel's day but for all time—is that God is firmly in control of *all* the world's events. You could also focus on this message by asking questions like these: *"How can I be sure that God is in control today? How can I have faith that God is in control of my life?*

Growing (35-40 minutes)
Read (optional)—Since the vision accounts in Daniel are quite different from the faith stories in Daniel 1-6, you might try reading the two chapters for this session in four parts: vision (7:1-14), interpretation (7:15-28), vision (8:1-14), interpretation (8:15-27).

Discuss—Use the following questions to supplement those in the General Discussion section. These questions aim to help bridge the gap from Daniel's beastly visions to the faith challenges surrounding us today.

- Daniel was probably in his late sixties when he had these troubling dreams. Why do you think God waited till Daniel was an older adult before sending these visions? In what ways does age affect our thinking about God's control over our lives?

- God gave Daniel not only visions but also heavenly interpreters to help explain them. How does God "interpret" the Word for us today? Who can help guide us in our understanding of God's will? Do we take full advantage of the help that's available? Why or why not?

- The angel Gabriel told Daniel that the vision of the ram and goat concerned "the time of the end" (8:17). Do Daniel's visions make you more or less anxious about the end of time and God's final judgment? Explain.

- It's clear from Daniel's dreams that God allows certain people and nations to run amok, deceiving and destroying even among God's people. Why would God allow such deception and destruction among the faithful? To what extent do such things teach punishment for disobedience, or even help bring people to faith? Think about and discuss current examples in which God has used hardship and persecution to spread and deepen faith.

Goalsetting (5 minutes)

In the coming week, keep an eye out for "signs of the end" such as those described by Jesus in Matthew 24. Where do you see enemies of God at work? Where do you see wars and rumors of wars? What natural events show that the creation itself has been deeply affected by sin? Be prepared to discuss how a greater awareness of these things can lead to a strengthening of faith.

Closing (10 minutes)

Preparing for Prayer—Read together Revelation 18:1-8 about the fall of Babylon. Take a few moments to think silently about the ways in which we participate in the deception and destruction of our own society. How does Daniel encourage us to live instead? Take some time also to mention personal concerns and praises.

Prayer—Turn next to Revelation 15:3-4 and read the words of the song there as the opening to your prayer. Continue by asking for the strength and courage to live by faith as we see human kingdoms rise and fall in this world. Everyone may join in to add other prayer items as well. Then close, if you like, with a familiar song of praise, such as "Great and Mighty Is the Lord our God" or "Now Blessed Be the Lord our God."

Group Project (Optional)
In our Scripture for lesson 8, Daniel begins by offering a prayer of confession on behalf of God's exiled people. Some of you may wish to gather prayers of confession from orders of worship, books of prayer, and other prayer resources. You might also like to try writing such a prayer of your own. Be prepared to use one of these at the beginning of your next study session. You could also make copies of prayers for others in the group to use during personal times of devotion.

*Daniel receives
not only visions
but visitors.*

8

DANIEL 9:1-11:1

God's Messengers

In a Nutshell

When Daniel offers a prayer of confession for the people of Israel, God immediately sends the angel Gabriel to deliver a response (Dan. 9). Then, a few years later, while Daniel is standing on the bank of the Tigris River, God sends a heavenly "man dressed in linen" to tell him about the future of his people. In both appearances, God's messengers bring Daniel a word of encouragement and strength. The prophet's testimony reminds all people of faith that God not only hears our prayers but also sends angels to work on our behalf.

Daniel 9

¹In the first year of Darius son of Xerxes (a Mede by descent), who was made ruler over the Babylonian kingdom—²in the first year of his reign, I, Daniel, understood from the Scriptures, according to the word of the LORD given to Jeremiah the prophet, that the desolation of Jerusalem would last seventy years. ³So I turned to the Lord God and pleaded with him in prayer and petition, in fasting, and in sackcloth and ashes.

⁴I prayed to the LORD my God and confessed:

"O Lord, the great and awesome God, who keeps his covenant of love with all who love him and obey his commands, ⁵we have sinned and done wrong. We have been wicked and have rebelled; we have turned away from your commands and laws. ⁶We have not listened to your servants the prophets, who spoke in your name to our kings, our princes and our fathers, and to all the people of the land.

⁷"Lord, you are righteous, but this day we are covered with shame—the men of Judah and people of Jerusalem and all Israel, both near and far, in all the countries where you have scattered us because of our unfaithfulness to you. ⁸O LORD, we and our kings, our princes and our fathers are covered with shame because we have sinned against you. ⁹The Lord our God is merciful and forgiving, even though we have rebelled against him; ¹⁰we have not obeyed the LORD our God or kept the laws he gave us through his servants the prophets. ¹¹All Israel has transgressed your law and turned away, refusing to obey you.

"Therefore the curses and sworn judgments written in the Law of

Moses, the servant of God, have been poured out on us, because we have sinned against you. [12]You have fulfilled the words spoken against us and against our rulers by bringing upon us great disaster. Under the whole heaven nothing has ever been done like what has been done to Jerusalem. [13]Just as it is written in the Law of Moses, all this disaster has come upon us, yet we have not sought the favor of the LORD our God by turning from our sins and giving attention to your truth. [14]The LORD did not hesitate to bring the disaster upon us, for the LORD our God is righteous in everything he does; yet we have not obeyed him.

[15]"Now, O Lord our God, who brought your people out of Egypt with a mighty hand and who made for yourself a name that endures to this day, we have sinned, we have done wrong. [16]O Lord, in keeping with all your righteous acts, turn away your anger and your wrath from Jerusalem, your city, your holy hill. Our sins and the iniquities of our fathers have made Jerusalem and your people an object of scorn to all those around us.

[17]"Now, our God, hear the prayers and petitions of your servant. For your sake, O Lord, look with favor on your desolate sanctuary. [18]Give ear, O God, and hear; open your eyes and see the desolation of the city that bears your Name. We do not make requests of you because we are righteous, but because of your great mercy. [19]O Lord, listen! O Lord, forgive! O Lord, hear and act! For your sake, O my God, do not delay, because your city and your people bear your Name."

[20]While I was speaking and praying, confessing my sin and the sin of my people Israel and making my request to the LORD my God for his holy hill—[21]while I was still in prayer, Gabriel, the man I had seen in the earlier vision, came to me in swift flight about the time of the evening sacrifice. [22]He instructed me and said to me, "Daniel, I have now come to give you insight and understanding. [23]As soon as you began to pray, an answer was given, which I have come to tell you, for you are highly esteemed. Therefore, consider the message and understand the vision:

[24]"Seventy 'sevens' are decreed for your people and your holy city to finish transgression, to put an end to sin, to atone for wickedness, to bring in everlasting righteousness, to seal up vision and prophecy and to anoint the most holy.

[25]"Know and understand this: From the issuing of the decree to restore and rebuild Jerusalem until the Anointed One, the ruler, comes, there will be seven 'sevens,' and sixty-two 'sevens.' It will be rebuilt with streets and a trench, but in times of trouble. [26]After the sixty-two 'sevens,' the Anointed One will be cut off and will have nothing. The people of the ruler who will come will destroy the city and the sanctuary. The end will come like a flood: War will continue until the end, and desolations have been decreed. [27]He will confirm a covenant with many for one 'seven.' In the middle of the 'seven' he will put an end to sacrifice and offering. And on a wing of the temple he will set up an abomination that causes desolation, until the end that is decreed is poured out on him."

Daniel 10:1-11:1

[1]In the third year of Cyrus king of Persia, a revelation was given to Daniel (who was called Belteshazzar). Its message was true and it concerned a great war. The understanding of the message came to him in a vision.

[2]At that time I, Daniel, mourned for three weeks. [3]I ate no choice food; no meat or wine touched my lips; and I used no lotions at all until the three weeks were over. [4]On the twenty-fourth day of the first month, as I was standing on the bank of the great river, the Tigris, [5]I looked up and there before me was a man dressed in linen, with a belt of the finest gold around his waist. [6]His body was like chrysolite, his face like lightning, his eyes like flaming

torches, his arms and legs like the gleam of burnished bronze, and his voice like the sound of a multitude.

[7]I, Daniel, was the only one who saw the vision; the men with me did not see it, but such terror overwhelmed them that they fled and hid themselves. [8]So I was left alone, gazing at this great vision; I had no strength left, my face turned deathly pale and I was helpless. [9]Then I heard him speaking, and as I listened to him, I fell into a deep sleep, my face to the ground.

[10]A hand touched me and set me trembling on my hands and knees. [11]He said, "Daniel, you who are highly esteemed, consider carefully the words I am about to speak to you, and stand up, for I have now been sent to you." And when he said this to me, I stood up trembling.

[12]Then he continued, "Do not be afraid, Daniel. Since the first day that you set your mind to gain understanding and to humble yourself before your God, your words were heard, and I have come in response to them. [13]But the prince of the Persian kingdom resisted me twenty-one days. Then Michael, one of the chief princes, came to help me, because I was detained there with the king of Persia. [14]Now I have come to explain to you what will happen to your people in the future, for the vision concerns a time yet to come."

[15]While he was saying this to me, I bowed with my face toward the ground and was speechless. [16]Then one who looked like a man touched my lips, and I opened my mouth and began to speak. I said to the one standing before me, "I am overcome with anguish because of the vision, my lord, and I am helpless. [17]How can I, your servant, talk with you, my lord? My strength is gone and I can hardly breathe."

[18]Again the one who looked like a man touched me and gave me strength. [19]"Do not be afraid, O man highly esteemed," he said. "Peace! Be strong now; be strong."

When he spoke to me, I was strengthened and said, "Speak, my lord, since you have given me strength."

[20]So he said, "Do you know why I have come to you? Soon I will return to fight against the prince of Persia, and when I go, the prince of Greece will come; [21]but first I will tell you what is written in the Book of Truth. (No one supports me against them except Michael, your prince. [11:1]And in the first year of Darius the Mede, I took my stand to support and protect him.)"

Are We There Yet?

Like several of the other chapters in Daniel, our passages for this lesson begin with a time stamp. It's the first year of King Darius's reign, approximately 539 B.C. This is the same Darius we met in Daniel 5:31 and in chapter 6. Even though he is identified as the son of a Mede named Xerxes, a name that figures prominently in the book of Esther, this is the earlier Darius who took over Babylon when Belshazzar was overthrown by the Medes and Persians (5:30-31). (See the section "In Search of Darius" in lesson 6. The events in Esther took place at least fifty years later.)

When the Medes and Persians took over, Daniel may have thought that the time for Israel's deliverance from captivity had come. He knew from his reading in the prophecies of Jeremiah that Jerusalem's desolation would be for a limited time. "This whole country will become a desolate wasteland, and these nations will serve the king of Babylon seventy years," the prophet had declared (Jer. 25:11; see also 29:10). Although a full seventy years had not yet passed, the Babylonians had been removed from power, just as Jeremiah had said: "'When the seventy years are fulfilled, I will punish the king of Babylon and his nation, the land of the Babylonians, for their guilt,' declares the LORD, 'and will make it desolate forever'" (Jer. 25:12). Daniel may have believed that the defeat of Belshazzar signaled a hastening of God's plans and that the captives would soon be released to return and begin rebuilding the city of David.

No doubt Daniel also remembered Jeremiah 29:11-14:

> "I know the plans I have for you," declares the LORD, "plans to prosper you and not to harm you, plans to give you hope and a future. Then you will call upon me and come and pray to me, and I will listen to you. You will seek me and find me when you seek me with all your heart. I will be found by you . . . and will bring you back from captivity. I will gather you from all the nations and places where I have banished you . . . and will bring you back to the place from which I carried you into exile."

Adopting appropriate signs of repentance—fasting, sackcloth, and ashes—Daniel approached the Lord in prayer.

Daniel's Prayer for the Nation

Daniel's prayer, a model of genuine confession, is seasoned with acknowledgments of God's love, righteousness, power, and mercy:

- "O Lord, the great and awesome God, who keeps his covenant of love . . ." (Dan. 9:4).

- "Lord, you are righteous . . ." (9:7).

- "O Lord our God, who brought your people out of Egypt with a mighty hand . . ." (9:15).

- "O God . . . we do not make requests of you because we are righteous, but because of your great mercy" (9:18).

Daniel was also very specific about the sins committed by the people of Israel, and he made no excuses for their lack of obedience:

- "We have sinned and done wrong. We have been wicked and rebelled; we have turned away from your commands and laws. We have not listened to your servants the prophets . . ." (9:5-6).

- "All Israel has transgressed your law and turned away, refusing to obey you" (9:11).

- "We have not sought the favor of the LORD our God by turning from our sins and giving attention to your truth" (9:13).

Notice especially that Daniel included himself in this litany of failure, making no attempt to set himself apart from the rest of the nation. This matter of accepting one's share of blame is rarely heard of in our society today. Instead, what we usually hear is that few, if any, people are even to blame for their own actions. Many of us blame our sins on our environment, or genetics, or peer pressure, or some other external factor. Others simply excuse their sinful behavior as their own personal expression or choice of lifestyle. Where there is no blame, how can there be the corrective feeling of shame? When people refuse to accept responsibility for their own actions, how can there be confession of sins?

Daniel's confession was unquestionably genuine. He acknowledged that he and Israel had received nothing more than they deserved. In fact, even in their exile God had been merciful, and it was only because of that great mercy that Daniel dared to come before God to ask for forgiveness.

A Quick Response

Even as Daniel made clear in his prayer that neither he nor Israel deserved God's mercy, he also stated that his petition was not for the benefit of the people but for the sake of God's name. And while Daniel was still praying, the angel Gabriel came to him "in swift flight" (9:21). Gabriel told Daniel that as soon as the prophet began to pray, an answer was given. So Gabriel came to give Daniel insight and understanding into this answer, which revolved around the number "seven" (9:24-27).

"Seventy 'sevens' are decreed for your people and your holy city to finish transgression, to put an end to sin, to atone for wickedness, to bring in everlasting righteousness, to seal up vision and prophecy and to anoint the most holy" (9:24). If we take "seventy 'sevens'" (noting that the original texts include no punctuation) to represent seventy times seven, or 490 years, we come close (as many interpreters have speculated) to the number of years between the date of the rebuilding of Jerusalem in the time of Ezra and Nehemiah (458-445 B.C.) and the date of Jesus' death and resurrection (around A.D. 30).

As tantalizing as that possibility is, we should also remember that Jesus himself used almost the exact same phrase, "seventy times seven," to convey the concept of completeness when he was speaking to Peter about forgiveness (Matt. 18:22; see also Gen. 4:24 for Lamech's notion of complete revenge). If this is the case here, Gabriel's message to Daniel is simply that God will bring an end to sin, usher in everlasting righteousness, and so on when God's time is complete.

Adding to the complication of interpreting the meaning of "sevens" is Gabriel's further declaration that there will be "seven 'sevens' and sixty-two 'sevens'" from "the issuing of the decree to restore and rebuild Jerusalem until the Anointed One, the ruler, comes" (9:25). This statement raises at least three possibilities:

- The prophecy refers to the rise and fall of Antiochus IV Epiphanes and his desecration of the temple (9:27; see 8:11-14, 23-26).

- The prophecy is about the Roman conquest of Jerusalem under the general Titus in A.D. 70.

- The prophecy will be fulfilled near the end of time (observe the many similarities between 9:26-27 and Matt. 24:4-25).

Again, as noted in earlier lessons, it's probably best for us to take the "both/and" approach. The prophecy was intended to be specific for those who read it originally, but it also contains an important message for each later generation of believers. In other words, the prophecy has been fulfilled in part but is yet to be perfectly completed. That fulfillment awaits the return of the Messiah, when Christ comes again and God's kingdom is complete in the fullness of time.

The Messenger Wore Linen

(Daniel's final vision in this book of prophecy begins in chapter 10 and continues into chapters 11-12, so we'll begin looking at it now—to focus on the messenger God sent—and we'll pick it up again in lesson 9.)

In about 536 B.C., a few years after receiving the vision of the "seventy 'sevens'" (Dan. 9), Daniel is given a revelation about "a great war" (10:1). We don't learn much about this war till it's described in more detail in Daniel 11-12, but at this early point we learn that there's also a spiritual war going on—and that it connects with the warfare between people and nations (see 10:13, 20-21; 11:1-12:3).

Daniel states that at the time he received this vision, he had been in mourning for three weeks—but we aren't told why. One possibility is that although Cyrus allowed the Jewish exiles to return to Jerusalem, Daniel may have been too old to make the trip. Whatever the reason, we can see that like Moses standing on Mount Pisgah, allowed to gaze into the promised land of Israel's future (Deut. 34:1-4), Daniel was given a spiritual glimpse into events that would take place in the future of God's people.

The messenger who came to Daniel is described in terms remarkably similar to those used by the apostle John when he received a vision of the Lord Jesus on the island of Patmos (Rev. 1:13-16). The messenger to Daniel was dressed in linen and wore a belt of finest gold (symbolizing royalty). His body was "like chrysolite" (yellow-green translucent stone), and his face was like lightning. What's more, the messenger's eyes were "like flaming torches, his arms and legs like the gleam of burnished bronze, and his voice like the sound of a multitude" (Dan. 10:5-6).

Despite the similarities in Daniel's and John's descriptions, we should bear in mind that the heavenly being of Daniel's vision was more likely an angel, not Jesus. This messenger spoke of being resisted by the prince of Persia (a reference to another spiritual being) and needing the help of "Michael, one of the chief princes" (10:13—referred to as an archangel in Jude 1:9 and Rev. 12:7). We will examine this spiritual conflict more closely in lesson 9.

Touched by an Angel

Whoever this messenger was, his appearance was terrifying—a fairly common occurrence in angel visits (see Num. 22:31; Josh. 5:14; Judg. 6:22-23; Luke 1:12-13; 1:30; 2:9-10). Daniel's strength left him, and he fell into a deep sleep (fainted? went into a trance?), with his face to the ground (Dan. 10:8-9). All the others who were with him, but who did not see the visitor, fled and hid themselves (10:7).

As he prepared to tell Daniel of things yet to come, the angel first touched Daniel and set him on his hands and knees (10:10). Calling Daniel "highly esteemed" (see also 9:23), the angel ordered the prophet to stand up. Then, after hearing what the messenger had to say, Daniel "bowed with [his] face toward the ground and was speechless" (10:15). The angel touched Daniel again, on his lips, and he could speak again (10:16).

Acknowledging his weakness in the face of this amazing vision, Daniel said, "I am overcome with anguish because of the vision, my lord, and I am helpless. How can I, your servant, talk with you, my lord? My strength is gone, and I can hardly breathe" (10:17).

Again the visitor touched Daniel and gave him strength (10:18). "Do not be afraid, O man highly esteemed," the messenger replied. "Peace! Be strong now; be strong" (10:19).

Strengthened further as the angel spoke to him, Daniel told the visitor to deliver the message (10:19). He was ready to hear about the future.

Additional Notes

9:3—Though fasting, sackcloth, and ashes were commonly understood signs of repentance, they do not make a confession genuine. In Isaiah 58:5 God declares, "Is this the kind of fast I have chosen, only a day for a man to humble himself? Is it only for bowing one's head like a reed and for lying on sackcloth and ashes? Is that what you call a fast, a day acceptable to the LORD?" In subsequent verses God makes clear that true repentance is seen not so much in symbols as in working against injustice and helping people who are poor and hungry (58:6-7; see also Mic. 6:6-8).

9:21—Gabriel's arrival "in swift flight" does not necessarily mean he flew with wings. The golden figures of the cherubim atop the ark of the covenant are depicted with wings (Ex. 37:9), however, and so are the seraphs in Isaiah's vision of the Lord as King (Isa. 6:2). Revelation 14:6 also describes an angel in flight.

10:1—There's a slight discrepancy between 1:21, which says Daniel "remained there until the first year of King Cyrus" (possibly referring to the end of the prophet's life), and this verse, which says Daniel received a revelation in the third year of Cyrus's reign. If the reference in chapter 1 refers only to Daniel's length of service in Babylon, he may have been working or retired in a different place (perhaps Susa?) at the time of this vision (see Additional Notes on 8:2 in lesson 7 about Daniel's tomb in Susa).

10:3—Daniel's note that he gave up meat and wine does not mean he had neglected his commitment to observing Jewish dietary laws (1:8). He may well have eaten meat if it was from an approved animal and was properly prepared. (See Additional Notes on 1:5, 8, 12 in lesson 1.)

10:5—The linen garment described by Daniel may have been like the clothing of a high priest (Lev. 6:10). The prophet Ezekiel also recounts a vision in which he sees a man dressed in linen (Ezek. 9:2).

10:7—The reaction of Daniel's companions was not unlike that of those who were with the apostle Paul when he had a vision of Jesus on the road to Damascus. On that occasion only Paul (Saul) saw the vision, even though the others were struck speechless (Acts 9:7).

GENERAL DISCUSSION

1. How would you react if someone told you that he or she had had an encounter with an angel? Would you believe that person? Why or why not?

2. What qualities in Daniel led both of his heavenly visitors to describe him as "highly esteemed" (Dan. 9:23; 10:11)? How would you feel if an angel said that to you?

3. In his prayer of confession, Daniel made clear that God always acted in righteousness, even in allowing the chosen people to be exiled (Dan. 9:14). Do we still perceive that God is perfectly just in all things? To what degree do we acknowledge our disobedience and its consequences? Explain.

4. Daniel's prayer was answered as soon as he began praying (Dan. 9:23). Why aren't all prayers answered that quickly? Why might God have us wait longer for the answers to some prayers?

5. What does the appearance of the "man dressed in linen" tell us about this visitor to Daniel?

6. The messenger explains that he was delayed twenty-one days, the same amount of time Daniel says he was in mourning (Dan. 10:2, 13). Do you think our experiences and even our emotions can be affected by unseen spiritual beings? Explain.

SMALL GROUP SESSION IDEAS

Opening (10 minutes)
Prayer—The optional group project at the end of session 7 invited people to write prayers of confession. If any of you did so, consider helping to begin this opening prayer time by sharing what you've prepared. Or you could read Psalm 51 together and spend some time in silence bringing your own private confessions to God.

Share—Take a few minutes to talk about the experience of confession. *How does it make you feel when you've confessed your sins? Are you tempted to make excuses for your behavior, or are you willing to accept responsibility? Do you ever wish you could share your confession with another person, as people do in some faith traditions?*

Focus—This lesson focuses on confession, God's response to prayer, and the heavenly beings God sends to convey messages and carry out God's plans. Consider this question as you move through this session: *If God sent Gabriel to speak to you, what message do you think the angel would bring?*

Growing (35-40 minutes)
Read—Since our Scriptures for this lesson are unfamiliar to many people, take the time to read them aloud together if some or all of you haven't already done so.

Discuss—Consider using these questions in addition to those in the General Discussion section.

- What's the relationship between humility, self-esteem, and godly esteem? Do you think it's biblical to encourage everyone to have high self-esteem all the time? Explain.

- How often do we include our nation (or even the church) in our personal prayers? What difference might it make if more believers made this a regular practice?

- Gabriel's message was not a very positive one, filled with wars and desolations. Would you want to know the future, even if it contained bad news? Explain.

- How do modern media images of angels compare with what we find in our Scriptures for this lesson? Why do you think the modern imagery developed the way it did?

Goalsetting (5 minutes)

Keep an eye out for evidence of angels during the coming week. If you can, bring along to the next session some examples of modern portrayals of angels. Do the portrayals honor these special beings? Do they accurately portray angels' roles in protecting and guiding God's people?

Closing (10 minutes)

Preparing for Prayer—This session began with an emphasis on confession. Consider closing with an emphasis on God's assurance of forgiveness. Read Psalm 103 together, and think about how these words apply to the Scriptures for this session. Also mention personal concerns and praises you'd like to bring before the Lord.

Prayer—Thank God for hearing our confessions, and for preparing an answer to our prayers as soon as we begin to pray. Ask for humility and for the grace to believe that even now there are heavenly beings all around us. Everyone may also join in with prayer concerns that have been raised.

Group Study Project (Optional)

The final two chapters of Daniel concentrate mainly on the period of history from Daniel's time until the second century B.C. persecutions under Antiochus IV Epiphanes. If you haven't already located or created a time line of that period (see group project at the end of lesson 1), perhaps you'd like to do so now. You can find help in a good Bible dictionary or handbook, a commentary on Daniel, or on the Internet. Then you could use your research as a visual aid during the final session of this study.

Group Study Project (Optional)

If you'd like to learn more about angels, we recommend *In the Company of Angels: What the Bible Teaches, What You Need to Know* by Andrew Bandstra (CRC Publications, 1995). A leader's guide for group study is also available. Call 1-800-333-8300 or visit *www.FaithAliveResources.org* for more information.

*Signs of hope
in times of
distress.*

9

DANIEL 11:2-12:13

Salvation Will Come

In a Nutshell

Daniel now receives a vision that describes the next two and a half centuries of Middle Eastern history. As we listen with Daniel, we realize that the vision describes our future too. In every age the people of God can have faith that the author of history is firmly in control of its future. The angel's closing words to Daniel apply to all who trust in the Lord: "At the end of the days you will rise to receive your allotted inheritance" (Dan. 12:13).

Daniel 11:2-45

2"Now then, I tell you the truth: Three more kings will appear in Persia, and then a fourth, who will be far richer than all the others. When he has gained power by his wealth, he will stir up everyone against the kingdom of Greece. 3Then a mighty king will appear, who will rule with great power and do as he pleases. 4After he has appeared, his empire will be broken up and parceled out toward the four winds of heaven. It will not go to his descendants, nor will it have the power he exercised, because his empire will be uprooted and given to others.

5"The king of the South will become strong, but one of his commanders will become even stronger than he and will rule his own kingdom with great power. 6After some years, they will become allies. The daughter of the king of the South will go to the king of the North to make an alliance, but she will not retain her power, and he and his power will not last. In those days she will be handed over, together with her royal escort and her father and the one who supported her.

7"One from her family line will arise to take her place. He will attack the forces of the king of the North and enter his fortress; he will fight against them and be victorious. 8He will also seize their gods, their metal images and their valuable articles of silver and gold and carry them off to Egypt. For some years he will leave the king of the North alone. 9Then the king of the North will invade the realm of the king of the South but will retreat to his own country. 10His sons will prepare for war and assemble a great army, which will sweep on like an irresistible flood and carry the battle as far as his fortress.

11"Then the king of the South will march out in a rage and fight against the king of the North, who will raise a large army, but it will be defeated. 12When the army is carried off, the king of the South will be filled with pride and will slaughter many thousands, yet he will not remain triumphant. 13For the king of the North will muster another army, larger than the first; and after several years, he will advance with a huge army fully equipped.

14"In those times many will rise against the king of the South. The violent men among your own people will rebel in fulfillment of the vision, but without success. 15Then the king of the North will come and build up siege ramps and will capture a fortified city. The forces of the South will be powerless to resist; even their best troops will not have the strength to stand. 16The invader will do as he pleases; no one will be able to stand against him. He will establish himself in the Beautiful Land and will have the power to destroy it. 17He will determine to come with the might of his entire kingdom and will make an alliance with the king of the South. And he will give him a daughter in marriage in order to overthrow the kingdom, but his plans will not succeed or help him. 18Then he will turn his attention to the coastlands and will take many of them, but a commander will put an end to his insolence and will turn his insolence back upon him. 19After this, he will turn back toward the fortresses of his own country but will stumble and fall, to be seen no more.

20"His successor will send out a tax collector to maintain the royal splendor. In a few years, however, he will be destroyed, yet not in anger or in battle.

21"He will be succeeded by a contemptible person who has not been given the honor of royalty. He will invade the kingdom when its people feel secure, and he will seize it through intrigue. 22Then an overwhelming army will be swept away before him; both it and a prince of the covenant will be destroyed. 23After coming to an agreement with him, he will act deceitfully, and with only a few people he will rise to power. 24When the richest provinces feel secure, he will invade them and will achieve what neither his fathers nor his forefathers did. He will distribute plunder, loot and wealth among his followers. He will plot the overthrow of fortresses—but only for a time.

25"With a large army he will stir up his strength and courage against the king of the South. The king of the South will wage war with a large and very powerful army, but he will not be able to stand because of the plots devised against him. 26Those who eat from the king's provisions will try to destroy him; his army will be swept away, and many will fall in battle. 27The two kings, with their hearts bent on evil, will sit at the same table and lie to each other, but to no avail, because an end will still come at the appointed time. 28The king of the North will return to his own country with great wealth, but his heart will be set against the holy covenant. He will take action against it and then return to his own country.

29"At the appointed time he will invade the South again, but this time the outcome will be different from what it was before. 30Ships of the western coastlands will oppose him, and he will lose heart. Then he will turn back and vent his fury against the holy covenant. He will return and show favor to those who forsake the holy covenant.

31"His armed forces will rise up to desecrate the temple fortress and will abolish the daily sacrifice. Then they will set up the abomination that causes desolation. 32With flattery he will corrupt those who have violated the covenant, but the people who know their God will firmly resist him.

33"Those who are wise will instruct many, though for a time they will fall by the sword or be burned or captured or plundered. 34When they fall, they will receive a little help, and many who are not sincere will join them. 35Some of the wise will stumble, so that they may be refined, purified and made spotless until the time of the end, for it will still come at the appointed time.

36"The king will do as he pleases. He will exalt and magnify himself above every god and will say unheard-of things against the God of gods. He will be successful until the time of wrath is completed, for what has been determined must take place. 37He will show no regard for the gods of his fathers or for the one desired by women, nor will he regard any god, but will exalt himself above them all. [38]Instead of them, he will honor a god of fortresses; a god unknown to his fathers he will honor with gold and silver, with precious stones and costly gifts. [39]He will attack the mightiest fortresses with the help of a foreign god and will greatly honor those who acknowledge him. He will make them rulers over many people and will distribute the land at a price.

[40]"At the time of the end the king of the South will engage him in battle, and the king of the North will storm out against him with chariots and cavalry and a great fleet of ships. He will invade many countries and sweep through them like a flood. [41]He will also invade the Beautiful Land. Many countries will fall, but Edom, Moab and the leaders of Ammon will be delivered from his hand. [42]He will extend his power over many countries; Egypt will not escape. [43]He will gain control of the treasures of gold and silver and all the riches of Egypt, with the Libyans and Nubians in submission. [44]But reports from the east and the north will alarm him, and he will set out in a great rage to destroy and annihilate many. [45]He will pitch his royal tents between the seas at the beautiful holy mountain. Yet he will come to his end, and no one will help him.

Daniel 12

[1]"At that time Michael, the great prince who protects your people, will arise. There will be a time of distress such as has not happened from the beginning of nations until then. But at that time your people—everyone whose name is found written in the book—will be delivered. [2]Multitudes who sleep in the dust of the earth will awake: some to everlasting life, others to shame and everlasting contempt. [3]Those who are wise will shine like the brightness of the heavens, and those who lead many to righteousness, like the stars for ever and ever. [4]But you, Daniel, close up and seal the words of the scroll until the time of the end. Many will go here and there to increase knowledge."

[5]Then I, Daniel, looked, and there before me stood two others, one on this bank of the river and one on the opposite bank. [6]One of them said to the man clothed in linen, who was above the waters of the river, "How long will it be before these astonishing things are fulfilled?"

[7]The man clothed in linen, who was above the waters of the river, lifted his right hand and his left hand toward heaven, and I heard him swear by him who lives forever, saying, "It will be for a time, times and half a time. When the power of the holy people has been finally broken, all these things will be completed."

[8]I heard, but I did not understand. So I asked, "My lord, what will the outcome of all this be?"

[9]He replied, "Go your way, Daniel, because the words are closed up and sealed until the time of the end. [10]Many will be purified, made spotless and refined, but the wicked will continue to be wicked. None of the wicked will understand, but those who are wise will understand.

[11]"From the time that the daily sacrifice is abolished and the abomination that causes desolation is set up, there will be 1,290 days. [12]Blessed is the one who waits for and reaches the end of the 1,335 days.

[13]"As for you, go your way till the end. You will rest, and then at the end of the days you will rise to receive your allotted inheritance."

As the World Turns

There's no denying that this final vision in the book of Daniel includes a lot of obscure historical detail. The vision portrays so many kings and armies that it's easy to lose track of who's who—and not one of them is given a name! It's almost like trying to watch a TV serial with the sound turned off. We can see the action taking place, but we have to do a bit of guesswork to sort out identities and relationships.

Fortunately we can compare the angel's description of events and characters with secular history and attach names to most of the individuals described. In the process we see an amazing degree of correspondence between the prophecy and the events that follow in history—so much so that some people believe this prophecy wasn't written until *after* the events had all taken place.

Before turning to the details of this vision, it might be helpful to think for a moment about why the angel didn't attach people's names to the events being described. This may be one of the strongest arguments in favor of believing this was a prophecy and not merely a historical account written *as if* it were a prophecy.

By withholding names and yet describing events in very specific terms, the angel made it possible for people like us, reading it many years later, to be convinced of the truth of the vision—noting various details that line up with events in history and recognizing also that the vision has yet to reach its ultimate conclusion.

When North Meets South

In Daniel 10 the angelic visitor said he had come to tell Daniel what was "written in the Book of Truth" (10:21). The angel had been fighting against "the prince of Persia" (10:20—a reference to another spiritual being; see 10:13) and was going back soon to continue the fight along with Michael, the "prince" of Daniel's people (10:13, 21).

From the time when Daniel saw this vision, there would be three more Persian kings—and then a fourth, who would be far richer than the others (11:2). It's hard to say which three kings of Persia the angel was referring to, since history records ten kings between the time of Cyrus and the victory of the Greeks. Of these, Darius the Great (522-486 B.C.—see Ezra 4:5, 24), Xerxes I (486-465 B.C.—see Esther 1), Artaxerxes I (465-424 B.C.—see Ezra 7:7), and Darius III (336-331 B.C.) played major roles. Xerxes I was known for his wealth and fought against the Greeks in 480 B.C., but it's more likely that Darius III was the final, wealthy king indicated by the angel, since he was the one defeated by Alexander the Great in 331 B.C.

Alexander is quite possibly the "mighty king" of Daniel 11:3, and after his brief rule and early death in 323 B.C., his kingdom was divided among four of his generals (see 11:4): Ptolemy I of

Egypt, Seleucus Nicator of Babylonia and Syria, Lysimachus of Asia Minor (modern-day Turkey), and Antipater of Macedon and Greece. Of these, the first two and their successors appear to figure most prominently in the rest of the prophecy. The division of Alexander's kingdom also confirms the angel's declaration that the descendants of the "mighty king" would not inherit his throne (Dan. 11:4): Alexander's half-brother and two children were all killed by the year 309 B.C.

The next part of Daniel's vision parallels the history of the Ptolemies and Seleucids, kingdoms of the south and north that fought for control of Palestine between 300 and 200 B.C. The king who became strong fits the description of Ptolemy I, and one of his former military commanders, Seleucus Nicator, became "even stronger" (11:5).

Their kingdoms became allies in 250 B.C., when Berenice, the daughter of Ptolemy II, married Antiochus II of the Seleucid line (see 11:6). One of the conditions of the marriage was that Antiochus II was to divorce his wife Laodice, preventing either of her sons from succeeding to the Seleucid throne. But Laodice had plans of her own, and after two years she arranged to have Antiochus II killed, along with Berenice's infant son. Berenice soon met the same fate, and Laodice restored her sons to the line of succession.

Meanwhile, back in Egypt, Berenice's brother, Ptolemy III, ascended to the throne and swore revenge against the Seleucids for his sister's death (see 11:7). Ptolemy III was successful in his campaigns, plundering his northern enemies and then leaving them to themselves for some years (see 11:8).

Perhaps Ptolemy III should have paid closer attention to the north, because soon Seleucus II came to power and waged war to the south (see 11:9-11). He was followed by Seleucus III and Antiochus III. Antiochus III was known as "the Great," becoming one of the most powerful of the Seleucid kings.

Little Big Horn

If you are getting confused by now (and believe me, you're not alone!), hang in there—you only have to know a few more details. Antiochus III (223-187 B.C.) and his vast Syrian army defeated the Egyptian Ptolemies in a series of battles (see 11:13-16). In an attempt to win control over the Egyptians, Antiochus offered his daughter, Cleopatra (the first of many queens in Egypt known by that name), to Ptolemy V (see 11:17). They were married in 194 B.C., but the marriage didn't bring about the hoped-for peace.

Antiochus III later attempted to conquer the territory in Asia Minor that once belonged to Lysimachus (see 11:18-19). He was defeated by the Romans (whose influence was growing at this time) and was later assassinated in 187 B.C. while trying to pay tribute to Rome—by means of robbing one of his own treasuries (see 11:19)!

Antiochus's son was an unremarkable king named Seleucus IV, who reigned from 187-175 B.C. (see 11:20). Seleucus's younger brother, however, was very remarkable. He was Antiochus IV Epiphanes (175-164 B.C.), who appears to have been the notorious "little horn" of Daniel 8:9-14 (see also 7:8).

Antiochus IV was not next in line for the throne. That honor belonged to his nephews. The exact manner of his rise to power is not clear (shrouded in "intrigue"—see 11:21), but once he was in power, his actions were well-documented.

In a brief time, Antiochus IV crushed all opposition, expanded his territory, and removed one of the high priests in Jerusalem (Onias III—see 11:22, a "prince of the covenant"). The many events listed in Daniel 11:23-39 are all incidents that characterize Antiochus's corrupt reign: buying friends with the spoils of battle (see 11:24); attacking Egypt, where his sister, Cleopatra, was now the queen mother (see 11:25); surviving dinner-table intrigue by his two Egyptian nephews (see 11:27); attacking Egypt again, only to be thwarted by naval vessels in league with Egypt (see 11:29-30); and desecrating the temple in Jerusalem on his way back to Syria (see 11:30-32; see also a detailed account in the apocryphal book 1 Maccabees).

Another important thing to recall is that during the last few years of Antiochus IV's reign, when the tyrant most oppressed the people of God in Jerusalem, the wide circulation of the stories and prophecies of Daniel encouraged faithful Jews to remain firm as they faced strong opposition.

From Here to Eternity

At Daniel 11:40 an interesting transition takes place. Suddenly we are no longer able to identify historical names and places with the various events being described in the vision. As we are told, the prophecy has advanced to the future "time of the end" (11:40). Shifting from the persecution of Jews under Antiochus IV, the vision now focuses on a coming persecution of believers under a final enemy, or antichrist, of God's people.

Daniel 12 opens with Michael, "the great prince who protects [God's] people," rising to defend the faithful (12:1). This picture illustrates the spiritual dimension of events that happen in the world of our experience. Just as the people of God on earth struggle to remain faithful against great opposition, so the angels of God struggle against evil spirits and powers that attack God's people.

The book of Revelation also describes spiritual combat in which God's angels battle the spiritual forces of evil on behalf of believers they protect on earth: "There was war in heaven. Michael and his angels fought against the dragon, and the dragon and his angels fought back" (Rev. 12:7). Although we do not often give much thought to spiritual battles being fought on our behalf, the Bible tells us enough about our protectors to encourage us to stand strong. We are not fighting on our own.

Salvation Will Come

Perhaps one of the most astonishing verses in all of the Old Testament—or at least in Daniel—comes near the end of Daniel's final vision. It's the promise of the resurrection: "Multitudes who sleep in the dust of the earth will awake: some to everlasting life, others to shame and everlasting contempt" (Dan. 12:2). Nowhere else in the Hebrew Scriptures do we find such a fully developed statement about the outcome of people's lives in the afterlife. The precise time of this end, however, is left unstated, just as in the New Testament (see Mark 13:32-33).

Daniel next saw two other visitors standing on opposite banks of the river (12:5; see 10:4), one of them calling to the man dressed in linen, "How long will it be before these astonishing things are fulfilled?" (12:6). As in Revelation, the answer reverts back to symbolism attached to prophecies about Antiochus and other enemies of God's people: "It will be for a time, times and half a time" (12:7; Rev. 12:14). While this phrase may refer to three and a half years, as some interpreters have guessed, it's more likely a "symbol for a limited period of unrestrained wickedness," as noted in the NIV Study Bible (see text note on Rev. 11:2).

Continuing, the man in linen declares, "When the power of the holy people has been finally broken, all these things will be completed" (Dan. 12:7). In other words, the end will come when God determines that the time of suffering and challenge for the people is complete (compare "until the time of wrath is completed"—11:36).

The vision closes with a statement of great comfort for all who have faith in God: "As for you, go your way till the end. You will rest, and then at the end of the days you will rise to receive your allotted inheritance" (12:13). After all the faith challenges, all the visions, all the numbers, all the history, all the persecutions—when all is said and done, this is the last word: *By faith the righteous will rise to eternal life.*

Additional Notes

11:2-39—It's important to be aware that different interpreters attach a variety of historical names to some of the characters described in this vision. Nearly all commentators agree, however, that the "contemptible person" mentioned in 11:21-39 is a reference to Antiochus IV Epiphanes.

11:22—The events surrounding the removal of "a prince of the covenant" are well described in the apocryphal book of 2 Maccabees. At least two priests attempted to buy the office of high priest from Antiochus after the removal of Onias III.

11:37—In the descriptions of deities here, the "one desired by women" is likely the male fertility god Tammuz (also associated with the Greek god Adonis). Tammuz is also mentioned in Ezekiel 8:14 when a heavenly visitor shows the prophet that idolatry is taking place within the temple.

12:1—Compare this "time of distress" in Daniel with the time of "great tribulation" mentioned in Revelation 7:14 (see also Rev. 12-13; 20:7-10).

12:11-12—A great deal of discussion has taken place about the meaning of "1,290 days" and "1,335 days." If taken literally, both of these measurements refer to a period a little longer than the apparent three and a half years ("time, times and half a time") of persecution prophesied in 7:25 (compare 12:7). The meaning of these numbers may have been clear to Daniel's first readers—and perhaps especially to those who underwent persecution in the second century B.C. For us, the message is simply one of hope and encouragement to remain faithful, because we know that the persecution of God's people will come to an end.

GENERAL DISCUSSION

1. What is the relationship between prophecy and faith? The prophecies in Daniel 11 and 12 cover the rise and fall of several kingdoms over hundreds of years. Are these prophecies as effective in encouraging people to remain faithful as the stories in the first half of Daniel are? How do prophecies affect our faith differently than stories do?

2. Most of the prophecies in Daniel 11 pointed to a specific time—the years between the end of Israel's captivity and the desecration of the rebuilt temple in Jerusalem in 168-167 B.C.—but they also have a message for our time. What lessons for today can we find in these passages?

3. The angel said that "the people who know their God will firmly resist" false teachers, tyrants, and other corrupting influences (Dan. 11:32). What are some ways in which people have sold out their faith today? What effect has this had on worship? With such strong cultural forces arrayed against us, how can believers remain faithful to God?

4. Daniel 12:1 reminds us again that the battle against evil is being fought not only here on earth but also between good and fallen angels (see 10:13, 20-11:1). In what ways, if any, does this affect your thinking about angels? How do you think guardian angels protect us?

5. In Daniel 12:2, 13 we find (somewhat as a surprise) references about the resurrection of the dead. How do you think Daniel's readers might have reacted to this idea? How strongly is this belief still held today? What kind of evidence shows that people believe in the resurrection to everlasting life?

SMALL GROUP SESSION IDEAS

Opening (10 minutes)
Prayer—As a prayer of gratitude for God's gift of the book of Daniel, consider beginning your prayer time by reading Psalm

16 (verse 8 could almost be a summary statement of Daniel's entire life). Ask the Holy Spirit for wisdom to understand God's meaning for us in Daniel's final vision, in which even the cast of characters can be confusing.

Share—Has anyone found or prepared a time line that depicts the series of kings and kingdoms following the Babylonian Empire? (See the study project suggestion at the end of session 8.) If no one has, perhaps one of you could make a list of these on a board or newsprint during this session.

Focus—Daniel's final vision focuses on God's control: over all of human history, and over the everlasting life we'll enjoy when earthly history is complete. Try keeping this question in mind throughout this session: *As I study Daniel's prophecies about the continuing course of life in this world and the promise of the life to come, how is my faith affected?*

Growing (35-40 minutes)

Read—The Scriptures for this lesson are long passages with a large cast of characters. So you may want to read a paragraph at a time, pausing in between to identify various parallels with Middle Eastern history a few centuries before Christ. Be aware that at Daniel 11:40 the prophecy shifts to portray events at the end of time.

Discuss—The following questions are designed to help everyone respond to the lesson material in a personal way as the group works through the questions for General Discussion.

- If an angel offered to tell you the general course of world history for the next few hundred years, would you want to know it? Why or why not? How could you use that knowledge to encourage people now or in the future to be faithful to God?

- Why do you think God allowed the Jews to be persecuted by Antiochus IV Epiphanes? What effect does persecution have on faith? (Consider Dan. 11:35.) Take a few moments to discuss some situations today in which believers are suffering under persecution.

- With the great sweep of history under God's control and with heavenly angels doing battle on our behalf, what prevents us from being mere pawns in some celestial game of chess?

- What lasting impression does Daniel leave on you? Does Daniel's example inspire you to live a more faith-filled life? Explain.

Goalsetting (5 minutes)

Take up the challenge of living in the world the way Daniel lived in Babylon. Even though much was foreign and even hostile toward his faith, he lived in line with God's Word. Take a few moments to list some of the ways our society works against us when we make a decision to live by faith. Commit together to resist temptations and to be faithful, in God's strength.

Closing (10 minutes)

Preparing for Prayer—Mention some things you've learned from this study of Daniel, and be prepared to thank God for them specifically. Try also to think of a one-word description of the thing you need most if you're going to keep living by faith. If everyone is willing, take turns sharing these one-word prayer requests. You may also want to share other concerns and praises.

Prayer—Read Psalm 16 (again) to begin your closing prayer. Thank God for all you've learned together while studying the life and prophecy of Daniel. Join in with any other prayer requests that have been shared. Then close, if you like, with a song of hope and faith such as "Lord of All Hopefulness" or "Rejoice, O Pure in Heart."

Group Project (Optional)

Some or all of you may be interested in a cause that looks ahead in faith, hope, and love. When God's kingdom comes in all its fullness, we will live with God; the earth will be restored; wars will cease; and pain, persecution, and suffering will be no more. The picture of resurrection to "everlasting life" in Daniel 12:2 points us to the great hope we have of living in God's presence forever. It also reminds us of ways we can serve in God's power to help bring the beginnings of peace and righteousness (justice) into our world today. For ideas and help in getting started on a project by which you can express your hope in Christ, check with health, welfare, political action, denominational, and environmental agencies.

For example, you could participate in a local immunization clinic, a blood drive, or a food program. Or you could help clean up a roadway, waterway, or disaster site. Or you could work toward human rights, legal justice, AIDS relief, community safety, literacy and basic skills education, biblical literacy, acceptance and education of mentally impaired persons, responsible medical research, preservation of wildlife, proper use of land, cleaner air and water—whatever you can think of. Every area of our lives and of this world is under Christ's authority, and he calls us to seek God's kingdom and righteousness even as we live in this world (Deut. 20:19-20; 22:6-7; Ps. 24:1-2; Matt. 6:33; Luke 12:31; Eph. 1:9-10; Rev. 22:1-2).

Evaluation

Background

Size of group:
- ☐ fewer than 5 persons
- ☐ 5-10
- ☐ 10-15
- ☐ more than 15

Age of participants:
- ☐ 20-30
- ☐ 31-45
- ☐ 46-60
- ☐ 61-75 or above

Length of group sessions:
- ☐ under 60 minutes
- ☐ 60-75 minutes
- ☐ 75-90 minutes
- ☐ 90-120 minutes or more

Please check items that describe you:
- ☐ male
- ☐ female
- ☐ ordained or professional church staff person
- ☐ elder or deacon
- ☐ professional teacher
- ☐ church school or catechism teacher (three or more years' experience)
- ☐ trained small group leader

Study Guide and Group Process

Please check items that describe the material in the study guide:
- ☐ varied
- ☐ monotonous
- ☐ creative
- ☐ dull
- ☐ clear
- ☐ unclear
- ☐ interesting to participants
- ☐ uninteresting to participants
- ☐ too much
- ☐ too little
- ☐ helpful, stimulating
- ☐ not helpful or stimulating
- ☐ overly complex, long
- ☐ appropriate level of difficulty

Please check items that describe the group sessions:
- ☐ lively
- ☐ dull
- ☐ dominated by leader
- ☐ involved most participants
- ☐ relevant to lives of participants
- ☐ irrelevant to lives of participants
- ☐ worthwhile
- ☐ not worthwhile

In general I would rate this material as

☐ excellent
☐ very good
☐ good
☐ fair
☐ poor

Additional comments on any aspect of this Bible study:

Name (optional): _____

Church: _____

_____

City/State/Province:_____

_____

Please send completed form to

Word Alive / Daniel
Faith Alive Christian Resources
2850 Kalamazoo Ave. SE
Grand Rapids, MI 49560

Thank you!